A Faith That
Touches the World

My special thanks to:

DAVID and MARY WEBB
IRIS HEAD
PAT FOX
VALERIE GOWER
RUSSELL BOWMAN-EADIE

This book is dedicated to all those courageous souls who lead Lent Groups

A Faith That Touches the World

A Lent Course

Edited by
JAMES JONES

with contributions from

Jim Thompson
David Hope
Nigel McCulloch
Vincent Nichols
Roy Williamson
Myra Blyth

Illustrations by Sarah John

DARTON · LONGMAN + TODD

First published in 1994 by
Darton, Longman and Todd Ltd
1 Spencer Court
140–142 Wandsworth High Street
London SW18 4JJ

Reprinted 1995 (twice)

ISBN 0–232–52042–9

A catalogue record for this book is available
from the British Library

Cover design by Sarah John

Phototypeset in 11/11½pt Times by Intype, London
Printed and bound in Great Britain
by BPC Wheatons, Exeter

Contents

Introduction

A Christian faith that does not touch the world is out of touch with the dynamic of God's mission. For, it was out of love for the world that God, the lover and giver of life, sent his Son Jesus Christ.

There are times when we in the Church seem so caught up with our own agenda for survival that we cease to connect with the world that we were destined to serve. A constant theme running through this course is the vocation of the local church to be faithful to its calling. So, it is appropriate that the setting of this Lent Course is in the local church.

When Jesus said 'I am the vine, you are the branches' (John 15:5) he made a remarkable statement about his relationship to his disciples. He did not say 'I am the trunk, you are the branches.' In styling himself as the vine he was making the point that just as the vine is the sum total of all the branches together, so Jesus Christ is to be seen in the gathering of his disciples. It is in and through the Church that Jesus becomes visible to the world. The same point is made by Paul when he writes, 'Now you together are Christ's body' (1 Corinthians 12:27). Although the Spirit of God is at work beyond the boundaries of the Church, the gathering of the disciples, it is clear from the Bible that within the providence of God the Church has a unique and high calling to be Jesus to the world, beloved of God, and to serve the world by witnessing to the reality of the Risen Christ, by preaching and living out the Good News and by singing to the glory of God the praises of him 'who called you out of the darkness into his wonderful light. Once you were not a people at all and now you are the People of God; once you were outside the mercy and now you have been given mercy' (1 Peter 2:9, 10).

But although the Church has a high calling from God it is clear from the New Testament that 'we are only the earthenware jars that hold this treasure' (2 Corinthians 4:7). The early Church wrestled with the same human frailty that we, two thousand years on, still contend with. Yet the Church is still here demonstrating that what has sustained it is 'an overwhelming power that comes from God and not from us.'

During this course we shall look often at the quality of these 'earthenware jars' and come face to face with their sheer ordinariness. Lent is an appropriate time for self-examination. But to look critically is not to look hatefully for we are not to despise what God has called into being and loves, his Church. It is important to remember that when we are led in this course to examine critically the Church and its mission we are bringing under scrutiny nobody but ourselves. It is too easy to make other people the scapegoats! Whenever we feel tempted to find fault with someone else it is a good Lenten discipline to start feeling for the plank in our own eye.

What emerges in these pages and interviews is that the future of Christendom depends, as it always has, on the power of God and on the vitality of faith that is expressed by local churches within their own neighbourhoods. It is fitting that

2

this should be the central theme of a Lent course pitched half-way through the Decade of Evangelism. Some have wondered whether a decade was too long to focus on evangelism. Leaving aside the truism that telling out the news that God loves the world is simply part and parcel of being God's people (in the Old Testament as well as the New), my own view is that given the speed at which many churches move ten years is just about right!

There is a momentum gathering and in many areas the tide has begun to turn. Nobody can deny that the task is daunting. The culture is changing before our eyes literally on the television screens. But this short book is offered in the conviction that the transformation and shaping of our culture after the image of God will be advanced not by grand schemes and national campaigns but by ordinary Christians in 'earthenware' churches engaging with and serving their local communities with the gospel of Jesus Christ. That's how the Church began. If faith is to touch the world, if the nations are to be evangelised, that is how it will happen again.

Suggestions for Group Leaders

Before the Group Meets Each Week

1. Listen to the cassette. (N.B. If the cassette-player has a counter put it to zero.)
2. Make a note of any comments by the contributor which you know your group would want to discuss.
3. Read the chapter in the book and make a note of anything that you think will interest the group.
4. Look at the passages and questions set. Do not be afraid to ignore these completely and devise your own questions and activities based on the interview.

   It is important to recognise that every group is unique with its own collection of experiences and its own chemistry.

   The material offered is not a strait-jacket but a means of enabling the group to reflect creatively on how their faith touches the world.

   Some groups will want to attempt to cover all the discussion material; others will be happy to do only one or two sections. Feel free to be flexible.
5. If you are starting the meeting with refreshments arrange for someone else to serve

them so you are free to welcome and to talk with people at the beginning. (N.B. If your group is coming together specially for this Lent Course then it is good to begin with refreshments so as to give people an opportunity of getting to know each other.)

6. An ideal number for a group is between eight and twelve.

7. It is important to indicate not only the time the meeting will start but also when it will end. (People new to the idea of joining groups are often nervous that they will be trapped.)

8. It is very important to check that the cassette player is in working order and audible for the size of the room, and that the cassette is at the right position.

9. Do ensure that each member of the group has a copy of the book. (Find out if there are any funds available to buy copies for those unable to afford them.)

10. Pray for your group and yourself that God will shed his light and peace on you all.

When the Group Meets

1. Seat everybody in such a way that they can all see each other's faces.

2. If people have come from different churches try to introduce them to one another.

3. Begin the session either with a time of silence or with a prayer (see the prayer on page 7).

4. Note those moments when the recorded interview produces a reaction from the group e.g. laughter, disapproval, quietness. These are points worth picking up in the discussion.

5. Don't hesitate to abandon your first question

by picking up something from the interview, e.g. 'People seemed to listen very attentively to . . . Why?'

6. Don't be afraid of silence especially immediately after the interview.

7. Give space to the quiet ones to speak but don't force anyone to contribute. Some people are very happy to leave discussion to others.

8. Don't hesitate to say to talkative members something like 'Thank you for that insight. I wonder if there's someone else who'd like to contribute to this . . .'

9. No matter how well the discussion is going *always* end the meeting at the time you have advertised. Meetings that go on and on soon lose the support of all but the garrulous!

10. When phrasing your own questions avoid 'Do you/Did you/Are you/Were you. . .' questions which elicit 'Yes/No' answers. Ask instead 'Why? To what extent? How?' questions.

After the Group Meets

1. If this is the first time you've ever led a group you'll probably be thanking God that it is all over!

2. After everyone has gone spend some time reflecting on the meeting noting the moments when it went well and those when it seemed rather hard. Ask yourself if there's anything you should do differently next week.

3. In your imagination go around the room and pray for each person by name that the light of Jesus Christ would shine on them and their church.

A Prayer
(for praying in the group before or after each session)

Leader: Lord
              lover of life
              giver of all
              circle the earth with your grace

All: And grant us a faith
              that touches the world

Leader: Lord
              lover of Christ
              giver of light
              circle the church with your grace

All: And grant us a faith
              that touches the world

Leader: Lord
              lover of us
              giver of peace
              circle this group with your grace

All: And grant us a faith
              that touches the world

Leader: Holy Father
              Holy Jesus
              Holy Spirit
              circle this place with your grace

All: And grant us a faith
              that touches the world.

The accompanying cassette may be obtained from booksellers or direct from:

> Bibliosound
> P.O. Box 1699
> Wells
> Somerset
> BA5 2YF

enclosing £6.90 (includes post and packing).

Session 1

Doubting the Disbelief

with Jim Thompson

Bishop Jim Thompson is well known through his appearances on the *Today* programme, presenting 'Thought for the Day'. He was affectionately nicknamed 'Big Jim' by the late Brian Redhead, an outstanding broadcaster, who recognised the Bishop's ability to communicate the Christian faith in words and sound-pictures. The Bishop's effectiveness in communicating lies in his realisation that not everybody finds it easy to believe in God.

I put it to him that the novelist Graham Greene had spoken about the impact Padre Pio, who manifested in his body the wounds of Christ, had had on his own doubts, that he had made him doubt his own disbelief. I asked Bishop Jim why he thought so many found it difficult to believe in God. He suggested that we have been through 'a sustained period of secularisation' where people felt that the universe was self-contained and that 'we were on our own in trying to cope with the earth. The obvious example is the spaceman who arrives in Mars and says that he can't see God up there. God has slowly been pushed to the very edges of our understanding. And this secular materialist propaganda has made it more and more difficult for people to understand and conceive of a God who is transcendent, who is living in his own dimension and relating to us.'

Given this tendency to believe only in the things that we can see and touch, the material world, he added that we are now a people who are alienated from understanding and believing in God in the way that people used to.

I asked the Bishop whether this was a subconscious thing. Did people choose to disbelieve? Or, to mix three metaphors, are we simply breathing in an atmosphere that clouds a belief in God? He answered the metaphors with an analogy!

Yes, it's rather as the adverts on television constantly change our way of thinking although we try to resist them. It is as though there has been a prolonged advert for not believing in God which is changing people's way of looking at it.

The Bishop identified another cause of today's disbelief.

I suppose the other main reason why people find it difficult to believe in God relates to the much more valid question against belief in God and that is the fact, the reality, of evil and suffering. And, of course, in the Bible in the book of Job the same question is asked. Job said, 'I am a good, righteous man and yet look at all this terrible suffering.' One of the other things that people find very difficult is that religion very often seems to play a very deep part in the existence of conflict and evil. I met someone recently in Northern Ireland who said, 'I can't believe in a loving God when all this is being done in the name of religion.' Of course, that's an over-simplification but that is a big reason, it's the biggest question that people come back to.

Evil and suffering have a paradoxical impact on faith in God. They operate like a piston. In one moment they drive you up towards God in search of answers and help; in the next, they pull you down and away from God in sheer disbelief, wondering how on earth a God of love could allow such suffering and evil. Yet suffering is a 'problem' only when people persist in a belief in God. If there is no God, suffering is just a fact of existence. It becomes a 'problem' only when we try to square it with the belief that the world is overseen by a good and loving God.

I took Bishop Jim back to the cultural climate dominated by the sciences which have given people an explanation of their lives without any reference to God and asked how the Church should respond.

We've lived almost all the time I've been a priest with two cultures. There's the culture which science produces. I don't think it's real science because if you consult someone like Einstein he sees great links between the way in which a scientist should approach the universe and the way people of faith do so with a sense of awe and mystery and imagination; that's the true essence of religion. We have to learn to understand that what we can't see, touch, prove (what he calls the impenetrable) really exists. And so, I have resisted very much the idea that somehow science and religion are set on collision course. All sorts of things are emerging. We have to face the facts; either the earth is a piece of shrapnel just speeding through the universe without purpose, meaning or direction other than from the explosion which sent it on its way; that's one way of looking at things and, if you really work that out in your life, it's quite terrifying and expects only stoic replies. Or, you think of it as an amazing act of creation in which the conditions for the earth to exist were precisely those involved in the original creation; then you're beginning to think about God and the wonder of God.

The point has often been made that religion and science are asking and answering two different questions. Religion asks 'Why?' and science asks 'How?' The way the Christian Church is to engage with a culture that is dominated by scientism is to press the questions of meaning and purpose which are beyond the sphere of science to investigate. Living on this planet we are like passengers cruising through space on a ship. Science may make the journeying (at least for some of the passengers) more intelligible and even more comfortable. It is religion and the Christian faith which addresses the issues of ultimate origins and destiny, meaning and purpose.

I asked the Bishop if he saw any other signposts of the existence of God that might challenge the prevailing climate of disbelief, that might make the atheist or the agnostic sit up and think again.

Well, I think that funnily enough for me one of the signposts has been the coming of people of other faiths to our land. I know that people are often very negative about other faiths. But there's something very deep about kneeling in a mosque with nearly a thousand men with their foreheads touching the ground in total obeisance to Almighty God. When you think that in our own society men in particular find God very difficult to cope with. They have this image that somehow God is a more feminine interest and a rather passive force. They are not at all sure that it's manly to be a believer. Now we may have things to be critical of in Islam, and in Sikhism but, on the other hand, within our secular state they have brought to us a vision of people who actually believe in the transcendent.

It is a frequent experience of clergy in our society that whenever they call on a home and the man opens the door, he always shouts for the woman in the house! It's a feature of our culture that the Christian religion is seen primarily as something for women. Certainly, women outnumber men as members of the Church. Why has the Christian faith lost its appeal to men? After all, the appeal of Jesus was as much to men as it was to women. Why has it become associated as something feminine?

I think it's partly because men resist suffering in a different way to women. I'm hopelessly generalising, of course, but I think it's a valid point. It has something to do with the characteristics in women which enable them to give birth which might necessarily just be brought out in the open by giving birth. I think also the hunting, the aggressive, the macho sides of human nature which have been very necessary to the survival of the human race are very deep within men. I think the religion of Christianity in particular with the suffering Saviour actually makes it more difficult for men who very often see their truth as being in control of things and to adopt a very positive and aggressive mode to life. The idea of passively standing silent before your accusers doesn't seem a very male idea to me. I also think we ought to draw out not the passivity of Jesus but the aggression of Jesus. You know he took on almost everybody in sight really. There's something about the way in which he calls the disciples which is very manly, you know, 'Come and follow me, I will make you fishers of men'. It's very direct stuff and I think sometimes we are too soft, too namby-pamby for men and they need a much more strong appeal followed up by end-

15

less argument because this is another thing – men on the whole are not keen to just accept truth as given.

Although the Bishop acknowledged the dangers of gender generalisation he pointed up the male characteristics that sit uncomfortably with our contemporary interpretation of Christianity: resistance to suffering, the necessity of aggression for survival, the ambition to be in control. If we persist in drawing out and emphasising the feminine characteristics in Jesus' life such as compassion, consensus, submission to suffering then it is unlikely that men already alienated from our churches will find Jesus appealing. Perhaps the men that are drawn to the Christian faith do so because they warm to a man who demonstrates the female virtues. But, those men who enjoy the company of other men because they reflect their own enjoyment of robust, adventurous, aggressive, argumentative experiences find the namby-pamby christology of 'gentle Jesus, meek and mild' not only unappealing but distancing.

The pity is that the vision of Jesus that turns many men away from Christianity and belief in God is only *one* of many other possible portraits. The Gospels furnish us with many features of Jesus' personality which are unashamedly male. He confronted and challenged his opponents, he joked with funny stories that sent people up, he raced around Galilee with a determination and single-mindedness that brooked no opposition, he loved the company of women and saw off those who were scandalised by the sight of a woman kissing his feet. Clearly there was a feminine side to his nature too. But twentieth-century western spirituality has painted a picture of Jesus almost exclusively in colours of feminine virtues. The portrait is incomplete. It has omitted the masculine contours of his body and personality so that when men have looked at the picture they have seen nothing of themselves. They've given it no more than a glance. Jesus and his God are not for them. So, I asked Bishop Jim if he agreed that we needed to stress the appeal of the adventure of Jesus.

I do, and of course, the whole emphasis on missionary work, of work amongst the poor, of the real demand-side of religion is much more important to men ... it's very interesting that men's groups are forming again because they need a special word spoken.

The image we have of Jesus will necessarily affect our vision of God. After all, Jesus is, as St Paul confessed, 'the image of the invisible God'. As we reflect upon him in the pages of the Gospels so the imagination comes into play, making present that which was in the past and calling to mind images of Jesus. His relationships, his actions, the pictures and stories in his teaching all provide us with the opaque glass, the window through which we stare and gaze at eternal truths. So, I asked Bishop Jim how we should go about stimulating the imagination in our pursuit of faith.

I think the creative religious imagination is one of the moribund faculties of the human race, particularly in this country. I believe we have got to open our imagination again and to think, as I've sometimes put it, 'to think eternity'; to realise that faith, if it's about anything, is about the relationship of our practical earthly life with God and with the angels, archangels and the whole company of heaven. The city of

God, the banquet of God: all these wonderful pictures which the Bible presents to us but which we've lost the capacity to understand and use for our own faith.

Western theology has become moribund in abstract concepts. Love, justice, mercy, righteousness, forgiveness, faith, redemption, sanctification: these are some of the worthy theological ideas that dominate Christian thought. But in concentrating on these concepts we have lost the art of the Master to tell stories and draw pictures that help ordinary people to see and to feel God. Jesus told stories to adults, not children. He never (so far as it is recorded) ever preached the abstract concept 'God is Love' although he did tell the most riveting stories about how God loved us, and in the most surprising ways.

Barren, abstract theological writing and preaching is a million miles away from the theology of Jesus. He told of God, his Kingdom and its virtues not in abstract terms of 'omnipotence', and 'sovereignty'. Rather he spoke of God who was like a good father or a landowner; he spoke of the Kingdom that was like a field or a tree; he spoke of virtue that was like a despised foreigner coming to the aid of an enemy. Jesus was able to draw people close to God because out of the richness of his own imagination he was able to paint pictures in words that appealed to the imagination of his audience. The chasm that exists between the Church and our culture is due in part to our failure as Christians to follow the Master in using the imagination in liturgy, teaching and evangelism.

Bishop Jim was clear about the importance of art and music in stimulating the imagination and, in particular, our awareness of God.

The great sacred music and sacred art play a huge part because in a way it carries the beliefs of the people who composed it. But I also think it's very important for us not to shy away from the great secular drama, literature, art. Because if you read the novels of Sartre, all the time they're showing you a world without faith in the godly sense. All these things ask us the right questions about our lives. And, I always feel, when reading works like that or looking at great works of art which have a lot of despair in them or which you know point to our inner loneliness and our angst, that what the poet and the artist and the musician are doing is really tapping into the questions we're asking. And, I always feel that they bring me to the point where I say – 'therefore God', 'therefore the gospel of Jesus Christ', because he is right where it hurts or where we're struggling to find answers.

I put it to the Bishop that, leaving aside the need to be more imaginative in the Church's liturgy and teaching and turning to the world of the arts, there seemed to be very few contemporary artists of note who were Christians. I wondered if it were easier to express and portray a world of despair. Could one communicate some reason, some purpose within the chaos of the modern world without appearing trite? I asked him if he felt that Christians often lack credibility with the world because they seem simplistic. Did he think that was a fair comment?

I think it is. It isn't just in art but in the whole area of life that it's very difficult to make Good News – News. Look at the average bulletin. As Martyn Lewis once said, 'We never have good news on the news' and it's the same with books. If you read great works by Dostoyevsky, for instance, they are full of suffering and sorrow all the way through and you might just get a glimpse of the Resurrection at the end. So, it is difficult. And, of course, in the past some of the art did seem to be hollow because it was being paid for by the Church! But the artists that mean a lot to me are those who really wrestle with the realities and come to their hope and faith through the realities of life. And it's so important that people do go on with the battle because we need our present-day *Missa Solemnis** to help us have a vision of what God's doing for the human soul.

I had been very taken by the Bishop's phrase 'to think eternity' and asked him what difference it made to have this outlook.

It first of all brings tremendous new vividness and meaning to our prayers. Because our prayers, like the Resurrection, like the Ascension, are the gate; they're the gateway, we stand at the gate between here and eternity. So, in adoring Christ we're actually trying to open up our soul to the dimension of God, to the heaven that surrounds us. 'Teach me, my God and King, in all things thee to see' [see p. 28] and it goes on to say 'who looks on glass', but then has 'to look through the glass and then the Heaven espy', so prayer becomes a totally different experience if you see it as you and God eternally. The other thing I would say which is in a way more direct and simple is that we all

* The solemn mass by such composers as Beethoven.

die. It's a great fact about our lives. And I have experienced this as a priest so many times; how faith in eternity produced at the last minute is pretty unreliable, but faith in eternity and living with eternity through long years has a wonderful way of sustaining you in the face of death. And death remains the greatest question mark over the human race. And I partly think that people have stopped believing because we have shied away from what our gospel offers. We believe in the whole company of saints, and we believe in the heavenly places and we believe in the great city of God in which people will be freed from hunger, grief, crying and tears. These are wonderful beliefs, yet we rarely offer them.

Death is the great leveller. In our attempt as Christians to be relevant, down-to-earth, practical and contemporary we have left out of the case the one item that might be of interest to those we visit with the gospel. The antidote to death. Without it society deals with its fears in its own way. Vitamin pills, health food, jogging, fibre, shell suits, hair-colouring, face-lifts are the elixir of extending youthful life. Ageing is a curse whose signs must be erased. Society does all in its power to dismantle every natural signpost that the path of life is terminal. Our death-dreading, no-hope-beyond-the-crematorium culture likes to pretend that ageing and dying are things that you can postpone. The fear of death stares you in the face from every shelf of vitamin pills and from every magazine rack promoting health and ageless beauty. Can the Church yet find a way of getting alongside its culture, of allowing people to face their fears therapeutically, of offering imaginatively a vision of heaven that is the antidote to death's dread?

Disbelief

1. Suffering, science and religious conflict were the reasons the Bishop identified for the lack of belief in God today. How far does that reflect your own experience of friends and family who find it difficult to believe in God?
2. These three areas continue to be issues for people of faith. What is it that sustains your own faith in the face of these difficulties?
3. If you can look back to a time when you did not believe in God, what was it that began making you doubt your own disbelief?

God in Creation

Read Romans 1:18–25:

> The anger of God is being revealed from heaven against all the impiety and depravity of men who keep truth imprisoned in their wickedness. For what can be known about God is perfectly plain to them since God himself has made it plain. Ever since God created the world his everlasting power and deity – however invisible – have been there for the mind to see in the things he has made. That is why such people are without excuse: they knew God and yet refused to honour him as God or to thank him; instead, they made nonsense out of logic and their empty minds were darkened. The more they called themselves philosophers, the more stupid they grew,

until they exchanged the glory of the
immortal God for a worthless imitation, *for
the image* of mortal man, of birds, of
quadrupeds and reptiles. That is why God
left them to their filthy enjoyments and the
practices with which they dishonour their
own bodies, since they have given up divine
truth for a lie and have worshipped and
served creatures instead of the creator, who
is blessed for ever. Amen!

Paul refers here to a wilful refusal to acknowledge
God. To what extent can we draw a distinction
between those people who won't believe in God
and those people who can't believe in God?
   How should people of faith respond to
(a)   those who won't believe in God?
(b)   those who can't believe in God?

Jesus the Man

1. What are the proportions of men and women
    in your church?
2. If there is a larger proportion of women than
    men, or men than women, how do you account
    for the imbalance?
3. To what extent do you agree with the view
    that the way we have presented Jesus has
    turned men away?
4. Read Luke 5:1–11:

    Now he was standing one day by the Lake
    of Gennesaret, with the crowd pressing
    round him listening to the word of God,
    when he caught sight of two boats close to
    the bank. The fishermen had gone out of
    them and were washing their nets. He got
    into one of the boats – it was Simon's – and

asked him to put out a little from the shore.
Then he sat down and taught the crowds
from the boat.

When he had finished speaking he said to
Simon, 'Put out into deep water and pay
out your nets for a catch'. 'Master,' Simon
replied, 'we worked hard all night long and
caught nothing, but if you say so, I will pay
out the nets.' And when they had done this
they netted such a huge number of fish that
their nets began to tear, so they signalled
to their companions in the other boat to
come and help them; when these came, they
filled the two boats to sinking point.

When Simon Peter saw this he fell at the
knees of Jesus saying, 'Leave me, Lord; I
am a sinful man'. For he and all his
companions were completely overcome by
the catch they had made; so also were James
and John, sons of Zebedee, who were
Simon's partners. But Jesus said to Simon,
'Do not be afraid; from now on it is men
you will catch'. Then, bringing their boats
back to land, they left everything and
followed him.

What was it about Jesus that attracted these
fishermen to him?

5.   Read Luke 7:36–8, 44–50; 8:1–3:

One of the Pharisees invited him to a meal.
When he arrived at the Pharisee's house
and took his place at table, a woman came
in, who had a bad name in the town. She
had heard he was dining with the Pharisee
and had brought with her an alabaster jar
of ointment. She waited behind him at his

feet, weeping, and her tears fell on his feet, and she wiped them away with her hair; then she covered his feet with kisses and anointed them with the ointment...

Then he turned to the woman. 'Simon,' he said 'you see this woman? I came into your house, and you poured no water over my feet, but she has poured out her tears over my feet and wiped them away with her hair. You gave me no kiss, but she has been covering my feet with kisses ever since I came in. You did not anoint my head with oil, but she has anointed my feet with ointment. For this reason I tell you that her sins, her many sins, must have been forgiven her, or she would not have shown such great love. It is the man who is forgiven little who shows little love.' Then he said to her, 'Your sins are forgiven'. Those who were with him at table began to say to themselves, 'Who is this man, that he even forgives sins?' But he said to the woman, 'Your faith has saved you; go in peace'.

Now after this he made his way through towns and villages preaching, and proclaiming the Good News of the kingdom of God. With him went the Twelve, as well as certain women who had been cured of evil spirits and ailments: Mary surnamed the Magdalene, from whom seven demons had gone out, Joanna the wife of Herod's steward Chuza, Susanna, and several others who provided for them out of their own resources.

What was it about Jesus that drew the women to him?

6. Look up Matthew 21:12–17.
What qualities in Jesus' character does this episode reveal?
To what extent could you define them as masculine or feminine qualities?

Faith and the Imagination

Read this famous passage from St Paul:

> When I was a child, I spake as a child, I understood as a child, I thought as a child: but when I became a man, I put away childish things. For now we see through a glass, darkly; but then face to face: now I know in part; but then shall I know even as also I am known. And now abideth faith, hope, charity, these three; but the greatest of these *is* charity.
>
> (1 Corinthians 13:11–13. Authorised Bible)

> When I was a child, I used to talk like a child, and think like a child, and argue like a child, but now I am a man, all childish ways are put behind me. Now we are seeing a dim reflection in a mirror; but then we shall be seeing face to face. The knowledge that I have now is imperfect; but then I shall know as fully as I am known.
>
> In short, there are three things that last: faith, hope and love; and the greatest of these is love.
>
> (1 Corinthians 13:11–13)

'The knowledge that I have now is imperfect'. Our knowledge of eternity and God is limited. It is through stories and images that we glimpse eternal truths. (The word 'darkly' (AV) and the phrase

26

'a dim reflection' (JB) translate the Greek word
enigma meaning a 'riddle' or 'story'.)

Keep a time of silence in the group and recollect
a story or picture or image from either the Bible
or literature or your own experience that has
enabled you to glimpse some aspect of God. After
the silence take time to pool your insights.

Fear of Death

1. What examples can you think of that show
   how our society is so ill-equipped to face
   death?
2. The Resurrection of Jesus Christ points to life
   beyond the grave. Why does it make such little
   impact in the modern world?
3. When you think about your own dying what
   do you most dread, most hope for?
4. Read Revelation 21:1–4:

   Then I saw *a new heaven and a new earth*;
   the first heaven and the first earth had
   disappeared now, and there was no longer
   any sea. I saw the holy city, and the new
   Jerusalem, coming down from God out of
   heaven, as beautiful as a bride all dressed
   for her husband. Then I heard a loud voice
   call from the throne, 'You see this city?
   Here God lives among men. He will make
   *his home among them; they shall be his
   people*, and he will be their God; his name
   is *God-with-them. He will wipe away all
   tears from their eyes*; there will be no more
   death, and no more mourning or sadness.
   The world of the past has gone.'

Think of a time when you wiped away the tears
from someone's eyes. Try to find one word to

describe the experience. This picture shows God wiping away our tears. Try to imagine it by keeping silent together in the group for five minutes. After the silence tell each other what you saw.

Teach me, my God and King

Teach me, my God and King,
In all things Thee to see;
And what I do in anything
To do it as for Thee.

A man that looks on glass,
On it may stay his eye;
Or, if he pleaseth, through it pass,
And then the heaven espy.

All may of Thee partake;
Nothing can be so mean
Which, with this tincture, 'For Thy sake,'
Will not grow bright and clean.

A servant with this clause
Makes drudgery divine;
Who sweeps a room, as for Thy laws,
Makes that and the action fine.

This is the famous stone
That turneth all to gold;
For that which God doth touch and own
Cannot for less be told.

(George Herbert, 1633)

Use this as a closing prayer. Ask one person to read it allowing a minute's silence in between each verse.

Session 2

God in Christ

with David Hope

The Right Reverend David Hope was principal of St Stephen's House, Oxford, then vicar of All Saints, Margaret Street in London before becoming Bishop of Wakefield, and now the Bishop of London. He brings to his episcopal ministry an experience of theological education rooted in the life of the parish.

When people begin to reach out beyond themselves, to explore the spiritual dimension to life they are faced with a confusing array of religious options. Not so much a supermarket, more a hypermarket of religions offering the consumer a range of spiritual choices. In the market-place of belief Christianity is but one of the many religious systems that the punter can choose. So how are we to characterise Christianity in relation to the others? Christian charity and principles of human rights make it wrong to belittle the faiths cherished by others. Yet the character of the Christian faith is shaped by the extraordinary and unique claims of Jesus Christ. Set alongside other teachers, gurus, prophets and spiritual leaders Jesus Christ is often described as 'unique' so I asked Bishop David how he would summarise the uniqueness of Jesus.

> That phrase 'the uniqueness of Jesus' is really a shorthand phrase. The word itself is a very compact and tight word for trying to explain or set out the special and particular person that we believe Jesus himself to have been. There's that word in the Old Testament, and brought again in the New, Emmanuel 'God with us'. And I think 'the uniqueness of Jesus' is actually saying: 'here we have the presence of God in Jesus'.

It was John Robinson, the Bishop reminded me,

who first spoke of Jesus as 'the human face of God'. In the person of Jesus, we see God's passion for justice, his heart of forgiveness, his longing to heal, his face-setting against evil and his love of life. Such was the integrity of Jesus' life with his message that those around him drew the conclusion that he was, as prophesied, 'Emmanuel', 'God with us'. But in the Old Testament 'Emmanuel' was a threatening word. It was used to warn people to behave themselves. 'Watch out! God is coming'. Rather like a mother might threaten an errant child with 'Behave yourself! Your dad will soon be home.' Yet in the New Testament 'Emmanuel' is associated with the name of Jesus and has a very different connotation. God is with us not to punish but *to save* his people from their sins, to forgive them. Herein lies the uniqueness of Jesus and the uniqueness of the Christian faith. Whereas in other religions there is the hope that God will one day forgive, here in Jesus Christ God has already given his pledge that he *is* our Forgiver, our Saviour. Forgiveness is a present experience not just a future hope.

Bishop David added that there was another dimension to the uniqueness of Jesus.

> Again, I think there is the unique way in which each of us experiences Jesus in our lives, the working of the Spirit in our lives. And you speak to different people and they each have their own unique, particular contribution to make in setting out their experience of Jesus.

I put it to the Bishop that Jesus gave the hardest time to religious people and that this makes very uncomfortable reading for people like us who are religious. Why was Jesus so hard on them?

I think probably because they deserved it as we deserve it! The sort of questions which Jesus asked, the challenges which he made, are challenges and questions which I think the Church today still needs to pay attention to, because so often we can settle down into the institution in a very cosy way, a very self-satisfied way. And at the heart of the Christian enterprise, I believe, is a very simple and straightforward question, an invitation of Jesus Christ, 'Come and follow me'. It's an invitation to follow *Jesus*. And, therefore, the Church, the Christian community or denomination (however you want to describe it), any collection of Christian people is less about an institution and more about relationships. And that's when you are at the sharp end of it, when we have to actually cope with each other, when you find yourself next door to somebody whom you actually don't take a particular liking to or you're not particularly cosy with. We are actually called to love one another.

Jesus never gave the commandment, 'Be ye nice unto one another'! The command to love each other in the way that he loves us is costly not cosy. In many churches relationships can be superficial. People can come and go on a Sunday, take part in a ritual but seldom engage in each other's lives. People can come to church hurting, weighed down with problems and leave without anyone noticing or, apparently, caring. Interestingly, many religious people seem happy to settle for this but outsiders who come can immediately sense the superficiality of the relationships and spot the hypocrisy of all the singing and preaching about love by those who fail to do it practically. When those outside the Church complain about the hypocrisy of religious people they find themselves keeping the company of Jesus who often berated religious leaders in the most strident terms. To call for the church to respond in earnest to the command of Jesus to love one another is not a cue for Christians to begin prying into the affairs of others or to suffocate others with cloying intimacy! A senior tutor at theological college once expressed the hope to some of his enthusiastic and ready-to-hug-anybody students that there would, at least, be some privacy in heaven! Yet to follow Jesus clearly involves us in living out the command to love one another at a level that is deeper than the superficial. 'Follow me' means to go after him into the wilderness, to go down on our knees in foot-washing service, to tread the road to Calvary and to walk through the valley of the shadow of death before we enter and dwell in the House of the Lord forever.

The Easter Event is central to the Christian religion. The death and the resurrection of Jesus, the suffering and the triumph, each provide a different focus. I asked Bishop David about the way some Christians get locked into presenting the Christian faith either as a perpetual Good Friday with an emphasis on the call to share Christ's suffering, or as a constant Easter Sunday with the exhortation to march through life triumphantly.

Well, I don't think it's possible to contrive a right balance. Some people may experience more of the Good Friday than of the Easter Day, others may experience more of the Easter Day than the Good Friday in their lives. My hunch is actually that for most of us there's

34

a kind of mixture of both those things, so it's not a matter of either/or. Our experience of life and of our Christian discipleship is that it is both/and rather than either/or.

Given that there are no adequate answers as to why God allows suffering, I asked the Bishop, what insights Good Friday gives us about the nature of suffering?

Certainly I think that there are sometimes simply no answers; we have to speak about the deep mystery of suffering and why that should be. But there is the cross, there is Gethsemane, the fact that God in Christ is with us, alongside us, within us and around us in human pain and suffering. He's not a God who remains distant from it all, he's deeply and intimately and painfully involved in our human experience in that way. Furthermore, I have been enormously humbled in my own ministry by my own experience among the sick where I have seen people in terrible pain and distress and yet discovering gifts of resilience, humour even, in some pretty desperate situations. And I have seen those who care for them, family, relatives, friends and the enormous courage and vitality in their endurance which has been evident; they discover gifts which they probably never knew they had.

It's almost now a truism of modern spirituality to say that God is with us in our suffering. But sometimes, and more often than not, when we suffer the feeling we have is that God is a million miles away. We can even feel that he must be punishing us for having done something wrong. In

35

what sense, I asked Bishop David, is God with us when the bottom falls out of our life?

> Well again you come back to the cross and to Good Friday because that's the heart of the paradox: God actually in Christ on the cross and yet Christ crying out, 'My God, my God, why has thou forsaken me?' And again, I think there's a mixture of both those kinds of extremes in a very painful conflict. Yes, people do say (I've heard it said), 'God's a million miles away from this.' And yet at the same time they perceive, in a way very difficult to describe, that the everlasting arms are there to hold them and to sustain them, so there's a kind of 'both/and' about it. There's a paradox at the heart of that.

The earliest gospel that the Church preached was that Jesus came into the world to save sinners. I asked Bishop David: 'How do we get this across in the twentieth century to a world that denies moral absolutes and even rejects the concept of guilt as some neurosis?'

> The world may do those things but I think it cannot escape the fact that there is evil around, in and amongst us as human persons. Read the newspaper headlines today; somebody has shot someone, rape, a whole range of wickedness and evil and I think it's simply not possible to escape from the fact that I personally am involved in that. And all of us at the end of the day do have, I think, some conscience about ourselves and there are guilty feelings about a whole range of things and I think we perhaps need to draw out those responses and those

feelings in others and see them for what they are.

Conscience is a soft and malleable faculty. Some can be too sensitive, others too callous. Conscience can be shaped by our upbringing or by the moral environment. It can be dulled by being ignored. It's not an infallible guide to right and wrong. Yet all human beings are conscious of a gap between what they are and what they ought to be. Sin may be an unfashionable word but universally people know the need of forgiveness. Such an experience acknowledges that there are some external and objective moral values that unite the offended and the offender. Morality is not simply some internal and subjective experience. At least, that is not how we behave. When conscience is outraged by some injustice and we call out for some action to end oppression we are behaving as if there were some morality that is binding on all people regardless of culture. When, for example, refugees in some far-off land are brutally slaughtered and foreign governments, condemning the outrage, demand a cessation of the violence on the grounds of justice, they are appealing to some external law that transcends culture and social conditioning. If morality were relative and purely a product of social conditioning, if conscience were simply a matter of personal preference, we would have no right to expect people from different cultural backgrounds to alter their behaviour. Logically, we would conclude that in the absence of absolutes we were just differently conditioned. But that's not how we behave. We speak and act as if there were absolutes. The Christian bears witness that there are; that what people intuit through their conscience is true; and that the source of these absolutes is God himself who expresses his moral character in the person of Jesus Christ.

Perhaps the Church today has conceded too easily, too quickly to the view that we live in a post-Christian society. The cry goes out that we live in a post-modern world where it is out of place for the Church to talk about moral absolutes. But there is no society on earth which holds that hatred is better than love, telling lies is better than speaking the truth, betrayal better than loyalty, breaking promises better than being faithful. Undoubtedly there has been a shift in social mores especially in the area of relationships but that does not obscure the truth that there are certain basic virtues which individuals and societies do perceive as absolute and binding for the continuing security of society itself.

It is against this yardstick that we examine our own lives. It is in our conscience that we feel the unease when we have failed. To hate, to lie, to betray, to break one's promise, these are some of the experiences that disturb the conscience and drive us in search of some release. If conscience is ignored its sound becomes muffled, dulled and, in time, mute. But, if its voice is heeded the person is ready to hear of the peace that can come to the troubled conscience through the forgiveness of God. It is through the cross of Jesus Christ that God offers such peace to the dis-eased soul. People may not talk so much these days of moral absolutes but the need of forgiveness is still widespread and deeply felt. It is to that universal experience that the gospel addresses itself.

As the Bishop of London, Bishop David presides over the Church of England in the nation's capital city. The City with its financial institutions and Westminster with the seat of government hold sway over the destiny of millions of citizens. As one of the senior bishops he sits in the House of Lords, so I pressed him on how we the Church are to get across the absoluteness of God-in-Christ to a society that would prefer to see religion and morality as personal and private experiences.

Bishop David replied in effect that we should remind people of the facts and let the facts speak for themselves.

> The way God has set us up is that we are social beings. The fact is that we do harm others whether we like it or not, that there is no action, no words which do not have an effect on other people. No person is an island. There is a huge interdependence. We rely on one another. We rub off against each other. And so inevitably, it seems to me, there must be a communality of values, of norms to which we ascribe.

One of the common values that people aspire to is the creation of a just society. Certainly, there are few people who, on the grounds of morality, would argue that we ought to make it more unjust! Everybody has a stake in society treating its members fairly. It is remarkable how even small children, no sooner have they learned to talk, begin to use the word 'fair'. True, it is more often to do with how they see themselves being treated; nevertheless there is in the young an acute and often accurate perception of what is fair and unfair. The creation of a just and fair society is again one of those absolute values that bind us together and show that we can overstate the case that society has abandoned all absolutes. All sorts of disparate groups – capitalists, socialists, demo-

crats, atheists, agnostics, Christians, Muslims –
agree on the desirability of working towards a
more just society. Politicians, of course, differ on
how to bring about such a society. It was Disraeli
who commented that political parties were like
two stage coaches travelling in the same direction
while spraying each other with mud! But, I put it
to the Bishop, as Christians should we not be
talking about something more than a just society?
The Kingdom of God reflects the character of
God. God is not only a God of Justice, he is also
a God of Mercy. The Kingdom of God should
surely be merciful as well as just. So, I asked him,
how do we go about creating a more merciful
society?

> Certainly mercy, compassion, forgiveness is at
> the heart of the gospel but it's not going to
> happen unless that is something in which I take
> an initiative personally. It's very easy to say
> they, the politicians, should be doing something
> about it. That's one of the problems I think
> these days. But we can't leave it, and shouldn't
> leave it, to the politicians. There is equally a
> personal responsibility on the part of Christian
> people for living the life of the Spirit, not being
> conformed to this world but being transformed
> in the power of the Spirit. Showing evidence
> of the gifts of the Spirit in our own lives of
> kindness, compassion, long-suffering, patience;
> all those things we're really so bad at but
> nevertheless we have to keep having a go at!
> I believe the Christian faith and the gospel
> actually challenge us all, politicians included.
> What I think we must be aware of is getting
> too closely involved in the party political dif-
> ferences and discussions. But actually the

Christian gospel speaks about the nature of God and the way God acts in our world and what he wills for our world in terms of justice, in terms of righteousness, in terms of fair dealing. Those messages are very clear in the prophetic tradition in the Old Testament for example. They are taken up in the Sermon on the Mount and in the whole teaching of Jesus. They still stand there as a clear challenge.

Many Christian leaders draw the distinction between being political and party-political. They agree that there are social and therefore political implications of ushering in the Kingdom of God, but they stop short of identifying or aligning the Christian gospel with any one political party. That may be the situation now but would that always be the case? I pressed the Bishop further. What about a political party that says that racism is a part of its manifesto? Surely then the Church ought to become party political in distancing itself from that policy?

There again the Christian tradition would really very strongly challenge such a statement and it would be right then for the Church, for Christian people, to stand up and make a protest about that.

I turned then to the issue of power. Christians have been very diffident about power. There's been great emphasis on Jesus identifying with the powerless to the point that powerlessness has almost become a virtue in some circles. But there can be no liberation of the poor without power and surely any study of Jesus from the Gospels shows him as an immensely powerful person?

Yes, indeed, there is great power and authority.

41

'All power and authority has been given to me in heaven and on earth' is a very extraordinary statement. But that is not the way he chooses to exercise his ministry. It's very clear that there is this exercise of power (again we're into a paradox) through powerlessness and actually becoming the servant of all, not lording it over others, not being at the top of the pile but at the bottom of the pile. And there's a model for the way it ought to be among those of us who are his disciples. I think there are some very clear lessons here for the Church, for the nature of those relationships about which we were talking earlier on and the ordering of those relationships. But the key to any kind of life and ministry in the churches seems to be basically that of service.

The Bishop went on to speak about the way the Church is called to wash the feet of God's world while at the same time fulfilling its vocation to challenge authoritatively those things which are clearly at variance with what God-in-Christ wills. In conclusion he gave an example of the Light challenging the Darkness in the modern world.

The Resurrection for me means the clear triumph and victory of God over the world. And perhaps it was most forcibly born in on me quite a number of years ago when I was in Bucharest in the very darkest days of the Ceauşescu regime. There on Easter night it was dark with the Securitate soldiers clustered around. And out of the darkened church the patriarch arrived with a big lighted torch. He shouted 'Christ is risen' and almost at once there was this huge cheer from the crowd. 'He has risen indeed!' And the whole square broke into light. That's the Resurrection of Jesus. The Triumph of Light over Darkness, the fact at the end of the day that God's word is the last word. Alpha and Omega. And I believe that with all my heart.

The Just and Merciful Jesus

Read Luke 4:16–22:

He came to Nazara, where he had been brought up, and went into the synagogue on the sabbath day as he usually did. He stood up to read, and they handed him the scroll of the prophet Isaiah. Unrolling the scroll he found the place where it is written:

The spirit of the Lord has been given to me, for he has anointed me.
He has sent me to bring the good news to the poor,
to proclaim liberty to captives
and to the blind new sight,
to set the downtrodden free,
to proclaim the Lord's year of favour.

He then rolled up the scroll, gave it back to the assistant and sat down. And all eyes in the synagogue were fixed on him. Then he began to speak to them, 'This text is being fulfilled today even as you listen'. And he won the approval of all, and they were astonished by the gracious words that came from his lips.

1. Spread around the group a pile of recent *local* newspapers. Get each person to cut out a story or picture for each of these categories:

43

(i) the poor (ii) the captives (iii) the blind (iv) the downtrodden.

2. After each person has presented their four stories/pictures ask what 'good news' would mean for:
(i) the poor (ii) the captives (iii) the blind (iv) the downtrodden.

3. To what extent would these people find 'good news' in or through your own church?

Just Mercy

Read Isaiah 1:11–18:

11'What are your endless sacrifices to me?
says the Lord.
I am sick of holocausts of rams
and the fat of calves.
The blood of bulls and of goats revolts me.
12When you come to present yourselves before me,
who asked you to trample over my courts?
13Bring me your worthless offerings no more,
the smoke of them fills me with disgust.
New Moons, sabbaths, assemblies –
I cannot endure festival and solemnity.
14Your New Moons and your pilgrimages
I hate with all my soul.
They lie heavy on me,
I am tired of bearing them.
15When you stretch out your hands
I turn my eyes away.
You may multiply your prayers,
I shall not listen.
Your hands are covered with blood,
16wash, make yourselves clean.

'Take your wrong-doing out of my sight.
Cease to do evil.
[17]Learn to do good,
search for justice,
help the oppressed,
be just to the orphan,
plead for the widow.

[18]'Come now, let us talk this over,
says the Lord.
Though your sins are like scarlet,
they shall be as white as snow;
though they are red as crimson,
they shall be like wool.'

Why was God offended by their religion?

What are the practical implications of verses 16 and 17 for your local church?

Receiving God's mercy opened up a new way of life. What difference does the experience of divine mercy make to a person?

Jesus – God With Us

1. In what ways would you say Jesus was unique?
2. The Bishop emphasised that everybody's *experience* of Jesus is different and unique.

    Complete the following sentence in no more than 15 words:

    'This is what Jesus Christ means to me ....'

    Share with the group the completed sentences.
3. The Bishop pointed up the difference between the church as an institution and the church as a relationship.

    Which word most accurately describes your own church?

(i) organisation (ii) club (iii) institution
(iv) building (v) family (vi) battlefield
(vii) community (viii) team (ix) school
(x) concert.

Circle your answer.

Underline what you think it ought to be.

What stops it moving from what it is to what
it ought to be?

The Suffering and the Triumph

1. The Bishop gave examples of when he had
   seen good come out of evil. What experiences
   have members of the group had of seeing good
   things arise out of tragic situations?
2. Jesus was one of us 'from the womb to the
   tomb'.

   Think of the Passion narrative.

   Make a list of the evil, sinful and treacher-
   ous actions that led to his execution. Then list
   what were the positive things that turned the
   sad day of his crucifixion into Good Friday?

The Servant God

Read John 13:1–17 **slowly**. As you do place yourself in the seat of Peter.

It was before the festival of the Passover,
and Jesus knew that the hour had come for
him to pass from this world to the Father.
He had always loved those who were his in
the world, but now he showed how perfect
his love was.

They were at supper, and the devil had
already put it into the mind of Judas
Iscariot son of Simon, to betray him. Jesus

46

knew that the Father had put everything into his hands, and that he had come from God and was returning to God, and he got up from table, removed his outer garment and, taking a towel, wrapped it round his waist; he then poured water into a basin and began to wash the disciples' feet and to wipe them with the towel he was wearing.

He came to Simon Peter, who said to him, 'Lord, are you going to wash my feet?' Jesus answered, 'At the moment you do not know what I am doing, but later you will understand'. 'Never!' said Peter. 'You shall never wash my feet.' Jesus replied, 'If I do not wash you, you can have nothing in common with me'. 'Then, Lord,' said Simon Peter, 'not only my feet, but my hands and my head as well!' Jesus said, 'No one who has taken a bath needs washing, he is clean all over. You too are clean, though not all of you are.' He knew who was going to betray him, that was why he said, 'though not all of you are'.

When he had washed their feet and put on his clothes again he went back to the table. 'Do you understand', he said, 'what I have done to you? You call me Master and Lord, and rightly; so I am. If I, then, the Lord and Master, have washed your feet, you should wash each other's feet. I have given you an example so that you may copy what I have done to you.

'I tell you most solemnly,
no servant is greater than his master,
no messenger is greater than the man
who sent him.

'Now that you know this, happiness will be yours if you behave accordingly.'

After reading the passage imagining yourself as Peter consider the following:

1. How did you react at the sight of Jesus kneeling in front of you?
2. What did it mean to you to hear Jesus saying, 'If I do not wash you, you can have nothing in common with me.'
3. This is the only time in the Gospels that Jesus ever calls himself 'Lord'.

   What light does this shed on Jesus' understanding of power and authority? and on our use of power?

Session 3

God in Me

with Nigel McCulloch

Bishop Nigel McCulloch oversees the Anglican diocese of Wakefield which he has unashamedly named 'A Missionary Diocese'. He has taken a leading part in the Church of England's strategy for the Decade of Evangelism with a passion to see more people become Christians.

I began by asking him whether there are any common experiences which mark the spiritual journey of every Christian.

I think the most important common experience is that every single one of us is different. I remember Cardinal Hume once saying that every person he met told him something different about God because every single person is made in the image of God. I think that's very important when we are talking about spiritual journeys, because it means that for every one of us there's going to be a different journey.

I find it fascinating when I've conducted confirmation services and I say to people, 'Now, what made you become a Christian? Why have you decided to be confirmed?' Some people tell me happy stories about it, because of the birth of a baby. Someone told me the other day about a mountain holiday in Austria and something about the awe-inspiring quality that led him to give his life to God. But I also find (and probably this is even more common) that it's when people have come against some terrible suffering: maybe it's a bereavement, or a baby's been born which is very sadly disabled; but somehow, against all the odds, in the darkness of that situation, the light has shone through. Rather than being turned away from God, they have found God, and committed themselves to Christ; and given their lives in a way that they themselves would probably never have expected to do.

Cardinal Hume's saying that every person he met told him something different about God may sound rather pious and hopelessly out of touch to somebody who's just been very badly hurt by someone. So I asked the Bishop whether he included rapists and terrorists amongst those who show us the image of God.

It was John Wesley who said that no-one is ever beyond the redemption of the Lord Jesus Christ. I would want to stick to that very firmly. I believe however bad people have been they are never beyond the forgiveness and the love of God. And if you really unpack it, you discover that a lot of terrible behaviour is actually done by people who themselves have been starved of love and forgiveness. This is one of the great and important things about our faith: that at its heart is that loving forgiveness of God.

The forgiveness of God is the touchstone of Christian experience. But how do we cope with that constant sense of our own failure as Christians?

Well I think failure is something that's very common. There's that lovely little jingle, 'If at first you don't succeed what a normal life you lead'! And I guess that is really perfectly true. I had an experience earlier in my life which helped me to understand this. I could never swim properly and for years people tried to teach me. I struggled so hard in that swimming pool! And then one day, when I was 24 years old, my neighbour took me into the swimming pool and actually taught me how to swim. The way she did it was to teach me to relax and to understand the power of the buoyancy of the water. And she was absolutely right, because once I had relaxed into the water, and felt it holding me up, then, without struggling, I was able to swim. I think that in all our failures, all our struggling, in life we must never forget that buoyancy of God's power which can hold us up.

The Bishop has a high profile in the Decade of Evangelism so I asked him about some of the theological approaches. I wondered whether it was right to lay such emphasis on Jesus or whether we should see Jesus more as a means of bringing people to the Father.

You know, I find that, personally, a difficult image. I know we're told about calling God our Father (daddy), and having that kind of intimate relationship we would have with a good father. But, you see, my father was killed in the war. I don't remember him at all. I was only 18 months old when he died. So I have never myself had any kind of example of fatherhood before me as I have grown up; and that's had its effect on my whole attitude to my faith. I find it very difficult to relate to somebody called a father. It's been much more authentic, from my point of view, to look at the life of Jesus and to remember that he said, 'He who has seen *me* has seen the Father' – seeing Jesus as the kind of person God wants us all to be; and then to understand the Father through that.

'Seeing Jesus' embraces a number of spiritual

53

experiences involving the sacrament, silence, meditation and worship. It extends to our relationships so that as well as imitating Jesus in the way we are to others we're encouraged by our Lord himself to find and see him *in* others and in the least of our brothers and sisters, the poor, the hungry, the prisoner and the destitute.

'Seeing Jesus', however, has its primary source in the Bible for it is with the Scriptures that we are able to evaluate our spiritual experiences. So, I asked the Bishop how important the Bible was in his own spiritual life?

I think that the Bible is absolutely the key to so much. But we've got to remember that our faith is not a faith of a book; it's about having faith in a person, in Jesus. I think that unless we study the Scriptures, we really don't understand all that God has to offer us. Jesus said, 'I come to give you life, that you may live it to the full'. I have found for myself, through things which I have come to know and love in the Bible, a real way of understanding the many different ways that God can work through so many different people. The Bible is a wonderful story of how God has brought his love to life on earth.

In the twentieth chapter of St John's Gospel is the story of Mary Magdalene on Easter Day. There she is in tears. It's very important to remember that joyous day of the Resurrection began in tears, because that is where many of us begin our deepest experiences in life. And the rainbow comes through the cloud. Then there's 2 Corinthians 4. Paul is talking about how in life we can get so easily battered and bruised. But the important thing is that, so long as we have our faith in Jesus, then we're never completely destroyed. That's been a favourite of mine for a long time and it was quite a surprise to me when I was consecrated a Bishop to discover that was the Epistle which is set for that service. I've come to realise why since I became a Bishop!

The Christian faith is bifocal in its seeing of Jesus. The Word is one lens, the Sacrament the other. The Eucharist, Holy Communion, is the centre of the devotional life of many Christians so I asked Bishop Nigel what we might expect of it.

I think that there are very many different ways of worshipping God. For a lot of people (and I know this because I used to be an organist in churches of different denominations) there are deeply authentic ways of worshipping God, which are not eucharistic. I have to say of course that, as an Anglican, the Eucharist is very much at the heart of my worship and my way of coming to know God. I think that service has about it a most important emphasis on hospitality and breaking of bread which takes us right back to the apostles; but also points us to what we are promised in the life beyond – which is a heavenly banquet with our Lord. Within the eucharistic service, the words which always speak to me very powerfully are those before the eucharistic prayer: when we are reminded that, with angels and archangels and all the company of heaven, we're taking part in our worship. For me, the Eucharist is a reminder, every time I take part in it, that we do belong both to this world and the next. We are never totally separated. We're one church: above and beneath.

One of the great influences in Bishop Nigel's life was the great hymn-writer Charles Wesley.

Without doubt, Charles Wesley had a very important influence in my spiritual journey. Earlier in my life, I found myself, in a sense, on a conveyor belt. I was one of those people who was brought up to go to church, and always carried on attending. I don't know if it was me, or an expectation placed on me, but everybody reckoned I was going to be a vicar. It was in my early twenties, when I was having to struggle with this myself, and feeling 'help, I want to get off' that I heard for the very first time the words that Charles Wesley wrote in the hymn 'O thou who camest from above', with its verse 'Jesus, confirm my heart's desire, to work and speak and think for thee'. I can say this really was a conversion experience, because at that moment I knew that was what God wanted me to do; and it was how I wanted to respond to him. It seemed as if God had been chasing me all my life; and at long last he'd got hold of me! Rather like when you're playing a game of Tic, you try to escape from being caught. When eventually you are caught, you are actually quite relieved! That's how it was with me.

O Thou who camest from above
The pure celestial fire to impart,
Kindle a flame of sacred love
On the mean altar of my heart.

There let it for Thy glory burn
With inextinguishable blaze,
And trembling to its source return
In humble prayer and fervent praise.

Jesus, confirm my heart's desire
To work and speak and think for Thee;
Still let me guard the holy fire,
And still stir up Thy gift in me:

Ready for all Thy perfect will,
My acts of faith and love repeat;
Till death Thine endless mercy seal,
And make the sacrifice complete.

(C. Wesley, 1762)

'Jesus, confirm my heart's desire to work and speak and think for Thee' echoes the longing of many Christians who make it their daily prayer. Although the hymn had been the means of God calling Bishop Nigel to ordained ministry I pointed out that there are, of course, many fully committed Christians who never become vicars!

They don't; and praise God that there are so many lay people who would sing that and feel it spoke to them. I do believe very strongly indeed that God's future for our Church in the next generations is going to be one where the lay people become, as the Lambeth Conference in 1988 described, 'the forefront missionaries of the Church'. And I see the job of people like myself as helping to teach and affirm and encourage the laity to go out into the world: among their families, in their street, wherever they may be, and be Christ in that situation. There's that lovely prayer of St Teresa of Avila, saying that Christ has got no eyes or hands or feet now, but ours. That's a great calling to any person, be they lay or ordained, to go out and be Christ in their world and see through the eyes of Jesus.

Although the Bishop was emphatic about the calling and sending out of the laity into the world to be salt and light, he nevertheless went on to stress the importance of the gathered community and of adding to its numbers.

I think that it's very important to encourage people to come and worship God. That's the prime reason for there being a Church. Six times in the Acts of the Apostles there's an emphasis by Luke on the number of people who had been added to the Church. So, I make no apology for being in the business of trying to add numbers to the worshipping congregations. When we do that we then have a more effective power base to go out into the world. I see any congregation which is worth its salt going out and being the salt in the world. But you can't be the salt unless you yourself are being made salty, if you like, by worshipping God and being strengthened by him.

In the course of our conversation it was clear that at the heart of his experience of God was the Bishop's awareness that all of us are responsible for our lives and answerable to God. This is a feature that is often ignored in modern spirituality. The emphasis on acceptance and self-esteem has led us to jettison all thought of God actually calling us to account both now and in the future. Although some old-fashioned images of God, such as Gerard Hughes' infamous Uncle George in *God of Surprises*, are rightly discarded, would it be a serious throwing out of the baby with the bath-water if we were to overlook completely a central strand of Jesus' own teaching which promised a moment of truth, a Day of Judgement for us all?

At the end of the day we all have to stand and face our Maker and give an account of how we've spent this life. I think that places into its proper context all the things that we are called to do as Christians. I often remember a poem which Geoffrey Studdart Kennedy wrote. It's a real favourite of mine. It's all about judgement and how this person goes up and has to face Jesus. The poem ends like this, 'There ain't no throne, there ain't no books. It's Him you've got to see. It's Him, just Him, that is the judge of blokes like you and me. And boys, I'd sooner frizzle up, in the flames of a burning hell, than stand and look into His face, and hear His voice say, "Well"!'

Given that the Bishop's life was so taken up with the Decade of Evangelism I asked him how the early gospel, about Christ dying for our sins in accordance with the Scriptures and on the third day rising again, related to the world on the brink of the third millennium.

I think, and I pray, that in the last five years of this century we really are trying to recapture our missionary verve, which we have lost for so long. The gospel of repentance is one that's very important and yet that is not a word that people like to hear. Sin is not a word people like to hear either. We are, most of us, people who are in need of a lot of love and forgiveness. People have become very wrapped up in themselves in this country; we've become a very selfish generation, really not caring too much about our neighbour. There is an enormous amount to be forgiven for, and to be loved for – as we move into a new millennium, with all the hopes that's bound to bring, and all the weird New Age religious views of those who try to cash in on this important moment. I'm not one of those bishops who personally doubts the rising of Jesus from the tomb on the third day. I believe what has been handed down through the Scriptures and tradition of the Church (though I have of course questioned it): what the Gospels say happened did actually take place; that Jesus was raised; and that when Mary Magdalene went to the tomb it was empty. I hope that as we move into a new millennium we'll have the courage of our convictions and be prepared to give this message of a loving and forgiving God who came to earth in Jesus Christ for every one of us.

In conclusion, I asked the Bishop for his own reflection on St Paul's description of 'the immeasurable greatness of God's power in us who believe'. Here is a grand statement about 'God in me'. To what extent can we expect to know God in this way? To what extent can we expect the same spiritual experiences as the first disciples who actually witnessed the Resurrection of Jesus?

I think part of the answer of that must be in prayer. We live in an instant society where we expect instant results. We tend to think that, if we organise things properly, then there is a good chance that they will happen. That's actually not the way of the Christian faith. We've got to have deep roots, and those deep roots are going to be the roots of prayer. We come to know God by taking time aside in prayer. For some people walking along a beach, or seeing a sunset is communicating with God. We've all got our different ways. It may be at the kitchen sink. But unless we take time to try and communicate with God then I believe our faith will be severely stunted.

One of the experiences which I look back on in recent years was an occasion in the church where I was a parish priest. A marvellous Steinway piano had been brought into the church, and a famous pianist was going to play on it. I enjoy playing the piano a bit myself. I crept into the church late that night. Nobody was about; and I started to play this piano. Now whether it was the acoustics, whether it was simply that this was a very special Steinway instrument, I don't know. But I made sounds that night more magnificent and more beautiful than I have ever made before. It seemed as if there was something which was greater than me enabling me to do that.

In a sense it was almost a little symbolic experience of God working through my rather ordinary little gifts. Every now and then (and this is true of all of us) God comes along and makes those gifts far greater than we really imagined. That little boy at the picnic when the five thousand were all there – he had just a few fish and a few rolls. Jesus took those and made them a banquet for five thousand. And he can take our little gifts and use them, and transform them, in a way far beyond what we could imagine.

Sowing in Tears

1. John 20:11–17:

Meanwhile Mary stayed outside near the tomb, weeping. Then, still weeping, she stooped to look inside, and saw two angels in white sitting where the body of Jesus had been, one at the head, the other at the feet. They said, 'Woman, why are you weeping?' 'They have taken my Lord away', she replied, 'and I don't know where they have put him.' As she said this she turned round and saw Jesus standing there, though she did not recognise him. Jesus said, 'Woman, why are you weeping? Who are you looking for?' Supposing him to be the gardener, she said, 'Sir, if you have taken him away, tell me where you have put him, and I will go and remove him'. Jesus said, 'Mary!' She knew him then and said to him in Hebrew, 'Rabbuni!' – which means Master. Jesus said to her, 'Do not cling to me, because I have not yet ascended to the Father. But go and find the brothers, and tell them: I am ascending to my Father and your Father, to my God and your God.'

The day of the Resurrection began in tears for Mary Magdala. As you look back on your spiritual journey what impact have times of sadness and sorrow had on your faith?

2. The Bishop quoted St Paul as a great encouragement. Read 2 Corinthians 4:7–11:

We are only the earthenware jars that hold this treasure, to make it clear that such an overwhelming power comes from God and not from us. We are in difficulties on all sides, but never cornered; we see no answer to our problems, but never despair; we have been persecuted, but never deserted; knocked down, but never killed; always,

wherever we may be, we carry with us in our
body the death of Jesus, so that the life of
Jesus, too, may always be seen in our body.
Indeed, while we are still alive, we are
consigned to our death every day, for the
sake of Jesus, so that in our mortal flesh
the life of Jesus, too, may be openly shown.

What person either from the Bible or from history
or from your own experience has been the greatest
encouragement and influence on your life of faith?

The Gift of Forgiveness

1. The Bishop said, 'If at first you don't succeed
   what a normal life you lead!' Here's how St
   Paul put it. Read Romans 7:21—8:2:

   In fact, this seems to be the rule, that every
   single time I want to do good it is something
   evil that comes to hand. In my inmost self I
   dearly love God's Law, but I can see that
   my body follows a different law that battles
   against the law which my reason dictates.
   This is what makes me a prisoner of that law
   of sin which lives inside my body.
       What a wretched man I am! Who will
   rescue me from this body doomed to death?
   Thanks be to God through Jesus Christ our
   Lord!
       In short, it is I who with my reason serve
   the Law of God, and no less I who serve in
   my unspiritual self the law of sin.
       The reason, therefore, why those who are
   in Christ Jesus are not condemned, is that
   the law of the spirit of life in Christ Jesus
   has set you free from the law of sin and
   death.

From this passage how does a person cope with
the tension of failing to live up to the standards
God expects of us?

2. Read Acts 2:37–47.

The early Church shared its message of forgiveness.
What were the features of their common life
that made their message so compelling to the
rest of the world?
What lessons are there to be learned here by
the modern Church?

Gifts in the Hands of God

The Bishop talked about God taking the gifts that
we offer and transforming them. Read John
6:1–15.

Some time after this, Jesus went off to the
other side of the Sea of Galilee – or of
Tiberias – and a large crowd followed him,
impressed by the signs he gave by curing
the sick. Jesus climbed the hillside, and sat
down there with his disciples. It was shortly
before the Jewish feast of Passover.
Looking up, Jesus saw the crowds
approaching and said to Philip, 'Where can
we buy some bread for these people to eat?'
He only said this to test Philip; he himself
knew exactly what he was going to do. Philip
answered, 'Two hundred denarii would only
buy enough to give them a small piece each'.
One of his disciples, Andrew, Simon Peter's
brother, said, 'There is a small boy here with
five barley loaves and two fish; but what is

that between so many?' Jesus said to them, 'Make the people sit down'. There was plenty of grass there, and as many as five thousand men sat down. Then Jesus took the loaves, gave thanks, and gave them out to all who were sitting ready; he then did the same with the fish, giving out as much as was wanted. When they had eaten enough he said to the disciples, 'Pick up the pieces left over, so that nothing gets wasted'. So they picked them up, and filled twelve hampers with scraps left over from the meal of five barley loaves. The people, seeing this sign that he had given, said, 'This really is the prophet who is to come into the world'. Jesus, who could see they were about to come and take him by force and make him king, escaped back to the hills by himself.

1. What was Jesus testing in asking Philip where they could get bread from to feed the crowd?
2. What immediately preceded the transformation of the bread and the fish? What does this teach us about how we should react in a crisis?
3. Consider quietly for a moment an occasion when you were made to feel very aware of the gap between the demands being made upon you and your own resources. How did you cope? If the stories are not too private share them with the group.

The Gift in Me

Jesus, confirm my heart's desire
To work and speak and think for Thee;

Still let me guard the holy fire,
and still stir up Thy gift in me.

1. What are the obstacles that thwart the heart's desire to work, speak and think for Jesus?

2. In worship and through prayer we find the gift of faith rekindled. But how do we turn our whole life (our working, our speaking and our thinking) into a way of prayer?

3. The Bishop said that in worship we 'belong to this world and the next.' We simply enter into that worship which is going on all the time in heaven with the angels.

   How might this truth affect the way that we approach our services of worship in church?

4. Return to the hymn 'O thou who camest from above'. Use it as a prayer. Let one person read it allowing a minute's silence between each verse.

   Alternatively, use a cassette of the hymn being sung and follow it with a time of silence.

Session 4

God in the Church

with Vincent Nichols

Vincent Nichols is the Roman Catholic Bishop in North London and Auxiliary Bishop to Cardinal Basil Hume. We met in Archbishop's House, Westminster, in a room that was in earlier days the Archbishop's bedroom. The topic of our conversation was God in the Church so I led off with the very predictable question: how would you define the Church?

I think the first point is that the Church is called into existence by God's initiative so there is an invitation from God to which we are asked to respond. So the Church is those who respond to the call of God. I think then in my understanding the Church takes a very concrete and specific form because that invitation is not just to an intimacy with God, but also with other people in a defined community of faith.

The Bible offers us a mosaic of different images to describe the people of God so I asked the Bishop which picture spoke most powerfully to him about what the Church is.

In the Acts of the Apostles, there is the account of people sharing common life and a fellowship of prayer and of concern for each other and for their material well-being. I think that's the description that speaks most strongly to me.

It is clear from the Acts of the Apostles that there was a missionary dimension to the Church right from the very beginning. So I asked then for his definition of mission.

I think in one sense you could say that the relationship between the Church and God is

69

almost like breathing in and breathing out. We breathe in, as it were, God's life and we breathe it out. So it is impossible to separate the call to a deep spiritual shared Christian life together as the community, the 'called' body, and the breathing out of those gifts in mission. So, I could never set the interior life of the Church in opposition to its mission because the two are as connected as breathing in and breathing out. I don't think we should be too narrow in coming to an appreciation of how the Church breathes out. I think the Church breathes out wherever people are inspired by the gospel, by their prayer, by the fellowship that they find in the gathered Christian community. In lots and lots of hidden unseen ways, people put their faith into practice: in a factory, in a launderette, in a kitchen, in conversation at the garden gate. These are people gently and humbly building the Kingdom of God.

Across the country in all denominations there are churches that are growing so I asked Bishop Vincent if he could identify some key features of a growing church.

Well, there are two. The first, I think, is a church where the life of prayer is vibrant, where people really do experience a sense of God's presence and a sense of shared faith. Now that can come in all sorts of different ways not least in how the worship, the liturgy, is celebrated in a parish. And the second characteristic is, I think, where a parish community is in touch with the hopes and the anxieties of the people who live in the neighbourhood. So it's got its feet on the ground and its eyes firmly fixed on Christ as Lord.

The Bishop noted the importance of the local church being in touch with the anxieties of people who live in the neighbourhood. An example of this is that many churches have grown through their contact with parents, children and families. This has happened without planning or a national strategy and has resulted in the mushrooming of family services and all-age worship which continue to grow in spite of criticisms from liturgical experts. Parents of young children, mostly mums, have found themselves isolated in the community. They've moved because of their partner's job and are cut off from the extended family network. Bereft of this support they feel alienated and vulnerable. When they discover that there's a local group of parents which meet during the week with activities for their energetic and demanding toddlers they're quick to join. It doesn't matter to them that this 'Parent and Toddlers' group is run by Christians. At the group they hear about a coffee-morning where the adults meet to chat about bringing up children, life, religion etc. and where the children are looked after in a crèche. It doesn't matter to them that sometimes they even discuss the Bible. In fact, it's quite intriguing. Then they hear that the local church has a service on a Sunday morning specially geared to adults with children and they've occasionally wondered about having the children 'christened' ... And so the story goes on until the children, the mother, sometimes the father and even some of their friends find themselves years later, and much to their surprise, active members of their local church. What has happened here is that the local church has been in touch with the bad news of that local community, namely the isolation and vulnerability of parents. By meeting people where they are and in the place where they are hurting the church can begin to share something of the Good News of Jesus Christ, about belonging to each other in a new way through belonging to God. In some communities this will be about touching the lives of alienated young people, in others about reaching out to the unemployed. Meeting people at their point of need is the way of sharing the gospel. Too often as a Church we have simply waited for people to come to us and wonder why they haven't. It simply hasn't seemed relevant to their anxieties or to their aspirations.

The Bishop developed the point further in respect of those parents who were concerned to provide a Christian education for their children.

So, for example, I think in our Roman Catholic tradition in this country we have placed great emphasis on trying to provide Catholic schools for the children of our families. Now, in one sense that can be interpreted as a rather narrow and defensive way of being present in a society. In another way though it's an attempt to address parents' most anxious longings and real hopes for their children, that somehow their children will grow up to share what they treasure and to make the most of their abilities and skills. And, in a sense, by putting so much effort into our schools it's almost as if we have provided the cement which holds together a parish. Often the school is the focal point of so much energy and outward activity.

The Bishop gave another example of the Church making connections with its local community.

In this part of North London people get

72

together to address pressing social needs, particularly in the areas in which the public services are missing or perhaps are being withdrawn. One example that comes to mind is where a number of parishes working ecumenically have got together to provide intermediate accommodation for people being discharged from psychiatric institutions. And I think there is a great sense of pride in those parishes that they are addressing, in a very down-to-earth way, a real and acute need. And they know they are doing it in the name of the church, they know they are doing it with the motivation of wishing to serve Christ in these people. I think the impact of that is very considerable.

Bishop Vincent's comment that the motivation of the Christians was of 'wishing to serve Christ in these people' reminded me of something Mother Teresa once said. When she was asked about the difference between what she did and the work of a social worker, she replied, 'Well, they do it for an idea and we do it for a person'.

Remembering that the Bishop had said that the relationship of the Church to mission was as close as that of breathing in and breathing out, I asked him what he considered to be the key aspects of liturgy in relationship to the mission of the Church.

Liturgy is so important and such a powerful moment in the life of the Church. Liturgy always introduces us to, and helps us to explore, our dependence on God because one of the great inhibiting factors in human life is when we believe that we are independent or self-sufficient. So I think that liturgy must always help us to face again that fact that we are not God, but that God is God and we come into God's presence asking for forgiveness.

I think there is a second thing that good liturgy does, and you see it sometimes in those desperate moments of tragedy and in those church services trying to bring people together after their lives have been shattered. Good liturgy gives meaning; it, at least, gives us a space to explore what does all this mean that has happened to us, either in tragedy or in great joy as with a wonderful wedding ceremony. It helps us to unpack layers of meaning in what we are engaged in our daily life.

The third thing that liturgy does is that it helps us to know and make plain that we are part of a long tradition. For example, Jesus' words 'Do this in memory of me' instantly link my experience with the whole of the Christian family that has gone before. I think that gives firmness and solidity. It gives authority to what we wish to do and who we are.

And, finally, I think good liturgy always ends with a sending out, with a mission, 'Go and do likewise'; this is the end of the mass, go and serve the Lord. And so there is an imperative that arises out of the very heart of good liturgy. Yes, these are the gifts we celebrate and it is ours now to share and to give.

When it came to asking the Bishop about the tension many churches feel between maintaining the fabric and its mission, he drew upon an example from Eastern Europe.

Not so long ago I was in the Czech Republic, and I visited a little village church just outside Prague which was in pretty poor repair but it was surrounded now by a huge housing estate of eighty thousand people. I said to the leader of this parish community, 'What are you doing to try and draw these people back to the practice of their faith? Are you appealing to their sense of history and tradition? Or are you appealing to their sense of solidarity in gathering together?' He said, 'No.' He said that in this estate the biggest problem was single-parent-families. 'Out of the community of 200 that go to mass every Sunday, we have got forty volunteers. And every doctor and every point of social reference on this estate knows that we shall have somebody there to help a single mother within hours of a telephone call'. And he added, 'Yes, we have got to repair the church, we have got to put it back into order, it's been neglected for forty years. But our priority must be that of showing, demonstrating the love of Christ in action in this community of ours.'

Everybody at some stage in their life reaches out towards God and at moments like that some do come to the Church. But often when they get there they find it's like a club. All the people know each other. It's very cosy. We are people turned in on ourselves who don't seem to be turned outwards ready to welcome the outsider in. How can we get over that problem?

It's difficult. It must be partly a greater sensitivity to those who happen to pass by, who drop into the church, who strike up a conversation with us on the tube. I sat waiting for the train one day and I was reading morning prayer out of a little book and this chap was sitting on the bench next to me. He said, 'Could I borrow that for a minute?' and I said, 'Yes, certainly'. He said, 'A friend of mine has just died.' I said, 'Just a tick, try that Psalm', and handed him the book. I think that moment was probably very important for him. I tried to persuade him to keep the book but he wouldn't. But I hope he takes the next step because he certainly was on a journey that was leading him to a more explicit and fuller faith in God. It's a terribly important ministry to have our churches open to give people an opportunity of popping in from the street and then somehow, with great gentleness and sensitivity, being alongside without ever pushing or intruding or haranguing or being too evangelistic in the worst sense of that word.

The picture of an ever-open church building sounded rather idealistic. Vandalism has forced many churches to shut. How did the Bishop envisage the Church maintaining his open-door policy?

I do think we are suffering slightly in the Church from what we have been talking about earlier: the separation of Church life and mission. And if we pull those two back closer together then it is a real missionary activity to have somebody in the church so that it can be left open, so that people can come by. That person, or team of people, can be there praying. This is a profound missionary activity. Now it mightn't be all day. But it's not beyond the wit of most parishes to devise a rota of people who will see it as their missionary activity to keep the church open, to make it a place of welcome and a place of prayer.

The Bishop was underlining a point that has been made strongly by Paul Avis that the Church, in this Decade of Evangelism, must make greater use of its own buildings as it reaches out to the community.

Absolutely. You look across the British landscape and every church that stands is a statement of meaning. It's a witness. It's part of the missionary activity of the Church to be there. Some years ago a young man in the middle of Liverpool 8 came and wanted to be married in the church. I said, 'Why in the church?' and I pressed him to find what his motivation was. He said with exasperation, 'Don't you understand,' he said, 'the very stones of this building are filled with people's prayers.' He knew that that church building was an important statement in society. It enabled him to link his moment of marriage into something which he knew was far greater than him. Now I don't think that maintaining and treasuring and making a church building available is the whole of the mission of the Church. But, nor do I think it should be opposed to the more active, socially orientated, kind of ministry.

In conclusion, I asked the Bishop about the Church and young people. Earlier, he had agreed that there was a sharp problem in that the Church continued to communicate in a way that was out of tune with the audio-visual culture in which young people were immersed. Young people find church boring not because they're not spiritual but because the language, music and culture of the Church are foreign to them. The average church serves you well if, in today's terms, you listen to Radio 4 and Radio 2. The language levels of the liturgy and the preaching are those of Radio 4 and the music often echoes the easy listening of Radio

2 unless you find yourself in a cathedral where you tune into Radio 3! Is the gospel to remain so narrowly limited? Do we have no mission to the audiences of Radio 1, Capital Radio, Virgin Radio and the plethora of regional radio stations? Are we to offer no other idioms with which people might seek and worship God? If not, then we are surely no different from those missionaries who went to far-off countries and insisted on building pseudo-Gothic churches in the middle of Africa and singing hymns from *Ancient and Modern*. The culture of young people who are unchurched needs to be taken seriously in the way that the missionaries always took seriously the host culture by learning its language, enjoying its heritage, listening to its fears, responding to its hopes and by communicating the gospel in their own idiom.

Bishop Vincent in agreeing identified another characteristic in the life of young people:

> I took a group of youngsters some years ago across Europe. First of all we stopped in Chartres and I said to them: 'You must look at this cathedral. It's one of the high points of medieval building and architecture and statement of Church.' So I walked gently round the outside and came back to discover most of them already in the bar. I said, 'Are you coming inside now?' 'Oh no, we've seen it, we've had enough.' But that same group, ten days later, I had to drag reluctantly out of the church at Taizé because somehow that building and the quality of relationships between the community and the young people was something living and so attractive to them. So I think we have to be prepared to put relationships in the Church first, worry less about

office. Then I think youngsters will find their way into the Church.

A Church at Worship

The Bishop identified four features of good liturgy:

  i. Dependence on God especially through forgiveness of our own independence.
 ii. Meaning, especially for times of tragedy and of joy.
iii. Tradition, the present being in touch with the past.
iv. Mission, being sent out to share and to give.

1. What other features would you add?
2. What examples can you give of when the liturgy has magnified one of these features either for you personally or for your church family or for your community?

A Church: Maintenance and Mission

1. The Bishop saw the relationship of the Church's life to its mission as one of breathing in and breathing out.

    To what extent does your own church imitate this natural rhythm of breathing?

2. The Bishop registered two facts in the growth of local churches: (i) Prayer (ii) Being in touch with the needs of the neighbourhood.

    To what extent is your church growing both in depth and in numbers?

    How far would you attribute its growth (or decline or remaining static) to these two factors (or the lack of them)?

3. The priest in the Czech Republic was in no doubt that mission took priority over the maintenance of the church's fabric. What practical difference would his policy make if applied to your church and neighbourhood?

A Church for the Young

Read Matthew 21:12–17:

> Jesus then went into the Temple and drove out all those who were selling and buying there; he upset the tables of the money changers and the chairs of those who were selling pigeons. 'According to scripture', he said, *'my house will be called a house of prayer*, but you are turning it into a *robbers' den.'* There were also blind and lame people who came to him in the Temple, and he cured them. At the sight of the wonderful things he did and of the children shouting, 'Hosanna to the Son of David' in the Temple, the chief priests and the scribes were indignant. 'Do you hear what they are saying?' they said to him. 'Yes,' Jesus answered, 'have you never read this: *By the mouths of children, babes in arms, you have made sure of praise?'* With that he left them and went out of the city to Bethany where he spent the night.

1. The young people were cheering Jesus in the Temple. The religious leaders were indignant. Why?
2. To what extent is this antipathy towards young people reflected in the Church today? Why?
3. How might your church go about turning itself

into 'a house of prayer for children and young people'?

4. What opportunities does your church have to receive and learn from children and young people?

A Church for All

Read Mark 11:15–19:

> So they reached Jerusalem and he went into the Temple and began driving out those who were selling and buying there; he upset the tables of the money changers and the chairs of those who were selling pigeons. Nor would he allow anyone to carry anything through the Temple. And he taught them and said, 'Does not scripture say: *My house will be called a house of prayer for all the peoples?* But you have turned it into *a robbers' den.*' This came to the ears of the chief priests and the scribes, and they tried to find some way of doing away with him; they were afraid of him because the people were carried away by his teaching. And when evening came he went out of the city.

Read Isaiah 56:6–7:

> Foreigners who have attached themselves to the Lord to serve him and to love his name and be his servants – all who observe the sabbath, not profaning it, and cling to my covenant – these I will bring to my holy mountain. I will make them joyful in my house of prayer. Their holocausts and their sacrifices will be accepted on my altar, for

81

>my house will be called a house of prayer
>for all the peoples.

The Temple was to be a House of Prayer not just
for the Jews but for all the peoples, for every race.
Therefore there was a courtyard of the Temple
specially set aside for the non-Jewish foreigner. It
was this area that was taken over by the money-
changers so that the foreigners were in effect
deprived of their opportunity of coming to the
House of Prayer. This made Jesus angry. The
Temple could not be called a House of Prayer for
every race. It was racism more than commercial-
ism that offended Jesus.

To what extent is your church a House of Prayer
for all the community?

How could your church become more a House
of Prayer for the whole community?

The Prayer of Teresa of Avila

Christ's Body

Christ has no body now on earth but yours;
   yours are the only hands with which he can
   do his work,
yours are the only feet with which he can go
   about the world,
yours are the only eyes through which his
   compassion
can shine forth upon a troubled world.
Christ has no body now on earth but yours.

Session 5

God in the Community

with Roy Williamson

One of the buzz words of today is 'community'. It's one of the great ideals by which virtues and vices are measured. Whatever undermines or wrecks a community is bad; whatever builds up the common life and makes for peace and harmony is good. A person who has wide experience of many different communities is Bishop Roy Williamson, formerly of Bradford and now of Southwark. If you're following this book with the cassette then you'll know from the sound of his voice that he has first-hand experience of the communities of Northern Ireland. So I asked him what he thought made a group of people a community?

In one sense it may be a geographical location. In another sense it may be a common purpose – a project, a particular line of action that might unite people together. Frequently, in my experience, it's a tragedy like the Bradford fire disaster or the Hillsborough soccer disaster. Certainly, when I was in Bradford at that particular time, a community which previously had been considered to be disparate suddenly overnight was united in grief. And they remained like that for a very, very long time in spite of the fact that just before that Bradford was seen as a divided city. But that common tragedy suddenly brought people together and they realised there was something here that they could share; not only sorrow but sympathy for those who needed it.

Although it is widely recognised that in western society we are highly individualistic there are times when we are enabled to transcend our own individuality. As the Bishop pointed out some of these moments we choose, others are just thrust upon us. Often it is suffering that binds a people together in a new and deeper sense of community. People open up to each other in their need; they share their stories of how the tragedy has affected them; they weep together. An example of this is to be found at the foot of the cross on Calvary. Mary, the mother of Jesus, and John, the beloved friend of Jesus, stand devastated as they see the one they love die before their eyes. Jesus in his dying moments gives them to each other in grief and through their tears binds them together in a new relationship, 'Woman, behold your son; son, behold your mother.' It is one of the redeeming dimensions of suffering that it releases in the human spirit the opportunity and the power to forge new relationships. But, I asked Bishop Roy, with reference to his experience of the tragedy in Bradford, whether the new-found sense of community could overcome some of the entrenched divisions of race.

Very much so. Because, indeed, it was the one thing which the immigrant community of Bradford were able to seize upon and I remember a group of them coming to me when I was actually drawing up the memorial service and saying, 'Look, this is our sorrow, this is our grief as well as yours. We came here thirty years ago. Our children have been born here. We share with you a common grief. We are part of this community.'

Community is an ideal that Christians cherish. Not just because Jesus commanded that we should love our neighbour as ourself but because the Christian understanding of God is as three-persons-in-community. To live up to the image of God means to live as persons-in-community. It is a relationship of mutual giving and receiving. In

the Gospel of John we have a partial drawing
back the curtain to glimpse this divine community
as we see the Father glorifying the Son, the Son
glorifying the Father, and the Spirit glorifying the
Son. As they give so they receive glory from each
other. It is not purely self-giving but giving and
receiving. Here is the perfect community by which
all human relationships are modelled and
measured. But in emphasising the Church as a
community do we not set up a tension between
her and the wider community, for the more we
encourage Christians to band together in the
Church the more we pull them away from involve-
ment in the community at large?

> Christians have a common purpose. And that
> common purpose is mission which actually
> turns them from being an inward-looking com-
> munity into an outward-looking community so
> the very fact that the Christian community may
> be emphasised should ultimately be for the
> benefit of the wider community. I believe that
> our church doors should, as it were, swing both
> ways. In fact in my family I have a joke that I
> would like bat wings on my churches' doors,
> like the old westerns, which swing in and out
> so that it is easy for people to get into the
> church and it's easy for them to get out of
> the church. Too often the church doors seem
> to me to be almost immovable. People can't
> get in, nor can they get out!

We in the churches don't make it easy for the
world at large to connect with us. The only time
that many churches are visibly humming with
activity is Sunday morning. The rest of the time
the doors are closed, mostly locked. The problem
is that on a Sunday morning the rest of the

world is lying in and never sees the church building alive. It's not surprising that some people find the message of 'Life in all its fulness' unconvincing!

Recently an engineer came to do some work on our church in south London which is in the Bishop's diocese of Southwark. I asked him if he'd ever done work in a church before and what it was like coming into a church building. He said it felt like entering a hospital. The comparison left me with mixed feelings. A hospital's a good image as a place of healing for the sick. But, it's also a very intimidating place for the ordinary person. Christians who don't think twice about going through the doors of their own church forget how alarming and overwhelming the whole experience can be for the outsider. We can easily be caught up with our own agenda – even for mission! – and totally ignore the real needs of those on the outside.

A businessman in sales and marketing was showing me the material he uses to enable his managers to see the importance of connecting with the needs and desires of their customers. He used the example of a hotel laying on a business meeting. The hotel's agenda consisted of providing flowers, lunch, ashtrays, coffee breaks, stationery and general comfort. The customer's expectations consisted of having telephones, fax machine, loos nearby, flexible coffee breaks, practical chairs and a spare bulb for the projector! There was a huge gap between the agenda of the hotel and the needs of its customers. Like a hotel the Church is there to offer hospitality to the traveller. Although the Church is not a business there's something to be learned here from the way that the hotel failed to meet the needs of those they thought they were serving. When seeing the Church as a community within the wider community we need to ask to what extent we are simply fulfilling our own agenda and how far that agenda is really being shaped by the needs of the wider community. Mission, as Bishop Roy says, is about being turned inside and out, about being sent for the benefit of others. We can only know what would benefit if first we have seen the needs.

Many communities in our country are identified not by geographical area or by a common concern, but by a faith that is different from Christianity. Given the Bishop's experience in two dioceses that are multi-cultural and multi-faith I asked him about the relationship between the community based on faith in Jesus Christ and the communities of other faiths.

> My own experience of this is that there is likely to be a greater openness towards other faiths and from other faiths if we are firm in our belief and our proclamation of what we believe ourselves. That's certainly been my experience in working with people of other faiths. They are much happier to relate to me if I have got a firm conviction about my own faith. The one thing they can't cope with or relate to is a faith which is vague, which you can't actually grasp hold of, and where there is no conviction in belief and proclamation of it. So, as I have engaged with Moslems, with Sikhs or with Hindus, they have never suggested that I soft-pedal my belief. They would actually want me to come out and state firmly where I stand. Then they found it much easier to relate to me and me to them.

I pressed the Bishop further because one of the

fears expressed by other faith communities is that the emphasis on the uniqueness of Jesus in this Decade of Evangelism might give oxygen to the racism that is endemic in all societies.

It really relates to that former question. I believe that if I am prepared to proclaim what I believe to be the uniqueness of Christ but proclaim it or teach it or share it sensitively and graciously then I get a hearing. Now there is a way of proclaiming Jesus as Lord which can sound dreadfully arrogant. For instance, if my Moslem, Sikh, Hindu, Buddhist neighbours hear me proclaiming Jesus is Lord and yet I don't live according to the teaching of that Lord ('Why do you call me Lord, and do not the things which I command you?'), then that is an arrogance and an inconsistency which they find difficult to cope with. But if I proclaim Jesus as Lord in such a way as to reveal that the Lordship of Jesus was seen in his vulnerability, that to my mind is at the heart of the uniqueness of Jesus, of Christianity and of God. That here we have someone who exercised his authority not by demanding that people do his will but by actually himself taking the lowest place and becoming weak and leading people in love rather than driving them in fear.

The Bishop sees the Church as keeping faith with its creeds, yet being open to other faiths and being the servant of all within the community regardless of their beliefs. He gave an example of how in a multi-faith situation he was able to speak unequivocally of Jesus as Lord while at the same time showing that vulnerability, which is characteristic of Jesus' life.

Yes, I saw it at the time of the Bradford fire. The service that we held was a memorial service. Into that service there were put elements from the Jewish, Sikh, Moslem and Hindu faiths as well as the Christian faith. And I was able to preach the Resurrection. I met with the leaders of the other faiths who were sharing with me beforehand and they were prepared to accept that. But it was done in such a way that didn't disenfranchise them. I was able to listen to their particular contributions and respect them. It happened on another occasion in a Bradford city football ground for the visit of Desmond Tutu. We were able to acknowledge together a great Christian leader who himself was vulnerable so often on the streets of South Africa, vulnerable before the power of the State. The inter-faith leaders of that city begged for the opportunity not only to come and listen but to take part and be on the same platform as this man.

Knowing the Bishop's evangelical roots in Northern Ireland and with the London City Mission I asked him whether or not he felt uneasy about taking part in the multi-faith worship of the memorial service in Bradford.

No, I didn't because in that sense it wasn't multi-faith worship. It was a Christian service into which we allowed and encouraged other people who were mourning and grieving. Contributions came from them that expressed their grief, that expressed their mourning, that expressed their sympathy. And that to me seemed to be a Christian thing to do. To allow them to do that.

The Bishop's faith and practice seemed to me to offer up new possibilities. Very often the inter-faith issue has been polarised into two camps. Some say that all we must do is listen to each other's stories of spiritual journeying; others argue that the only biblical way forward is to preach the gospel to people of every faith and none. What Bishop Roy seemed to be advocating was not an either-or but proclamation in the context of genuine dialogue and conversation.

That would be a very fair description but there is another thing I would like to add. As well as dialogue and proclamation I think there is service to the community. I think that people of all faiths can actually get together to serve the local community. I believe that people of all faiths can come together to challenge the evils in our society from their own faith perspective. I believe people from other faiths can come together and speak about shared values, for example concerning the family and children. We've got so many things in common as people of faith. We can get hung up on the proclamation and the divisive dialogue sometimes, whereas there are many things that can actually unite us. And as we serve together we can learn from each other.

My mind immediately goes to the story of the Samaritan woman at the well. She has this conversation with our Lord, 'Well, you know, our Fathers worshipped on this mountain and you say that Jerusalem is the place that we ought to worship.' At no time at that point is Jesus dismissive of her. He actually does her the courtesy of listening to her. Now he goes on to point her to the true way but he is not dismissive. I believe that there are many instances in the Scriptures and in the history of the Church where if we are not dismissive of people then we can actually go a long way to sharing our faith with them. As long as we have the courtesy and the integrity to believe that there are some things that they have to share with us.

Bishop Roy is committed to a vision of society always in the process of being reconciled within itself. But I challenged him about the Church ever being an instrument of that reconciliation when it was so often full of disagreements and conflict.

There is a sense in which the Church can only have credibility in speaking about reconciliation if it itself has known division and conflict. The fact that we are all sinners and the fact that we have this treasure in jars of clay and, therefore, all the time we are wrestling against circumstances and problems is bound to produce conflict. And the Church is not immune to conflict. Because we feel things so deeply as Christians there are bound to be differences of opinion. So there is a sense in which it's only out of conflict that we can speak with credibility about reconciliation. But I have to say that if the Church goes on without resolving its conflicts I do think it has a detrimental effect upon its message of reconciliation. And so in my homeland of Ireland where there are certainly as many churches as there are pubs (and that's saying something) nevertheless the Church is deeply divided. And in that situation it is very difficult for the gospel to have any credibility in the eyes of the community. And the same is true, of course, in places like

Bosnia and other parts of the world where the depth of religious division is frightening. I guess at the end of the day we can only speak reconciliation with credibility when we are seen to be wrestling with our own divisions and taking action to resolve them. And in all those situations that I have mentioned, in Bosnia and in Ireland, there are glorious little incidences and illustrations of people across the religious divide actually saying, 'enough is enough', and we are going to link hands. I visited a little Columbian community right in the middle of the troubles in Belfast and there were there just ordinary people, most of them lay-folk, who had formed this little community across the religious divide. They weren't able to do very much except be a testimony to the power of reconciliation in Christ.

The New Testament shows us the reality of the early Church as a group of people together in Christ working through their difficulties. It was Spurgeon who advised a young man in search of the perfect church that when he found it he shouldn't join for he would only spoil it!

The unity of the Church begins at its points of disagreement. The supernatural element is manifest not through everybody agreeing with each other, but with the way that people hang in there together sometimes resolving, sometimes simply living with their differences. The Church is a remarkable institution for there are very few organisations that bring together, for example young and old. Where, I wonder, beyond the confines of a family circle do young and old today enjoy each other's company? Of course there are tensions in every church. But to be in Christ together means that in our common allegiance to him we are bound to each other. At the end of the day we kneel nakedly honest before the same cross, we come each of us in need of forgiveness to the same Saviour. There's no place for superiority on the hill of Calvary.

Moving from divisions in the Church to divisions in society I pressed the Bishop to spell out the role of the Church in a world where the chasm between rich and poor was growing daily. I drew attention to the fact that the Government was handing back into the private and the voluntary sector more of the caring in the community, for example for the elderly and the mentally ill. The Church, of course, is responding to this in some places in a magnificent way providing a safety net where there is none. I asked Bishop Roy to what extent he thought that the Church was going back to what it was several hundred years ago and becoming almost an alternative social service?

Yes, it's almost as though the wheel has turned full circle really. The Church was a great educator and healer in days gone by and it is coming back to that. Now I think there are two things I want to say about this. The first is, I think, the Church needs to stand up against the State and challenge the State if it is not actually fulfilling its responsibilities. So often the Church perhaps hasn't done its homework properly in the things that it's said to the State about these things. But I think we must get our act together and be prepared to speak intelligently to the State about those areas where we feel it is actually letting people down and not fulfilling its responsibilities. Secondly, if we are reaching a stage where the State is either unable or unwilling to exercise its responsibilities in certain directions then there is no reason why the Church ought not to be in the vanguard of actually picking up the slack and in the name of Christ caring for people. Let the Christian values shine out through helping the mentally ill, serving the homeless and so on.

The Bishop clearly envisages both a pastoral and a prophetic role for the Church in relation to the State. So, as a bishop who sits in the House of Lords, did he think that the Church's prophetic vocation to speak on behalf of the vulnerable and the marginalised was aided or compromised by the Church of England being established?

I believe that the Church being established in this country certainly has a better platform for that kind of prophetic statement. But I would not go to the stake for establishment because at the end of the day we have such a person as the Holy Spirit who, if the Church is empowered by the Spirit, will be able to make the prophetic statement whether the Church is established or not.

It seemed to me that the Bishop might be hedging his bets! I drew attention to the danger of dividing everything between the sacred and the secular, as if only certain things, i.e. the Church belonged to God. Does not the establishment of the Church make the point that it is all one kingdom, that the Church and the State, together under the symbol of the Crown, come under the kingship of God? If you disestablish the Church you end up giving credence to the view that on the one hand you've got the secular which is the

State and on the other hand you've got the sacred which is the Church. In other words, the State is the realm of human affairs and the Church is the realm of spiritual affairs and never the twain shall meet. Does not the establishment of the Church stand as a symbol through which we see the integrity of the sacred and the secular as one kingdom under God?

> Certainly one of the reasons why I am not in the vanguard of those wishing to destroy the establishment is because I actually think that the establishment does make the very point that you have made. The withdrawal, for instance, of the Church from being the established religion of the country and the withdrawal of, for instance, the bishops from the House of Lords would actually make a statement which may become so loud in the ears of some people as to be interpreted as the Church washing its hands of the State, washing its hands of the secular things and simply dashing for refuge behind its closed doors.

There is no doubt that when bishops and archbishops speak out on issues of public concern they capture the headlines precisely because they occupy a position within the establishment. If the Church were relegated to the sidelines as a sectarian religion it is unlikely it would command the attention of the media which is so vital in making its prophetic voice heard beyond the ranks of the converted. For all the drawbacks of establishment the established Church, speaking ecumenically and in harmony with leaders of other faiths, has the opportunity of being what Bishop Roy calls 'the arbiter of the nation's spiritual conscience'.

Church and Community

1. What is it that makes your church a community?
2. To what extent is your neighbourhood a community? What is it that makes it such?
3. Which of these five diagrams most reflects the relationship of your church community to the wider community of your neighbourhood?

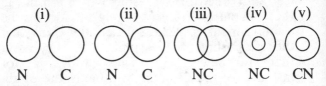

| (i) | (ii) | (iii) | (iv) | (v) |
| N | N   C | NC | NC | CN |

[N = Neighbourhood]   [C = Church]

4. List in two columns:
   i. the priorities of your local church,
   ii. the needs of the neighbourhood.
   To what extent do these two lists correspond to the diagram you chose in 3?

Other Faiths and God

Read Acts 17:16–34:

> Paul waited for them in Athens and there his whole soul was revolted at the sight of a city given over to idolatry. In the synagogue he held debates with the Jews and the God-fearing, but in the market place he had debates every day with anyone who would face him. Even a few Epicurean and Stoic philosophers argued with him. Some said, 'Does this parrot know what he's talking about?' And, because he was

preaching about Jesus and the resurrection, others said, 'He sounds like a propagandist for some outlandish gods'.

They invited him to accompany them to the Council of the Areopagus, where they said to him, 'How much of this new teaching you were speaking about are we allowed to know? Some of the things you said seemed startling to us and we would like to find out what they mean.' The one amusement the Athenians and the foreigners living there seem to have, apart from discussing the latest ideas, is listening to lectures about them.

So Paul stood before the whole Council of the Areopagus and made this speech:

'Men of Athens, I have seen for myself how extremely scrupulous you are in all religious matters, because I noticed, as I strolled round admiring your sacred monuments, that you had an altar inscribed: To An Unknown God. Well, the God whom I proclaim is in fact the one whom you already worship without knowing it.

'Since the God who made the world and everything in it is himself Lord of heaven and earth, he does not make his home in shrines made by human hands. Nor is he dependent on anything that human hands can do for him, since he can never be in need of anything; on the contrary, it is he who gives everything – including life and breath – to everyone. From one single stock he not only created the whole human race so that they could occupy the entire earth, but he decreed how long each nation should flourish and what the boundaries of its territory should be. And he did this so that all nations might seek the deity and, by feeling their way towards him, succeed in finding him. Yet in fact he is not far from any of us, since it is in him that we live, and move, and exist, as indeed some of your own writers have said: "We are all his children".

'Since we are the children of God, we have no excuse for thinking that the deity looks like anything in gold, silver or stone that has been carved and designed by a man.

'God overlooked that sort of thing when men were ignorant, but now he is telling everyone everywhere that they must repent because he has fixed a day when the whole world will be judged, and judged in righteousness, and he has appointed a man to be the judge. And God has publicly proved this by raising this man from the dead.'

At this mention of rising from the dead, some of them burst out laughing; others said, 'We would like to hear you talk about this again'. After that Paul left them, but there were some who attached themselves to him and became believers, among them Dionysius the Areopagite and a woman called Damaris, and others besides.

1. Paul engages here with people of different beliefs. How does he react to their sacred monuments?
2. To what extent does his quoting from a different religious tradition offer guidance to Christians in their attitude to sacred texts other than the Bible?
3. Paul recognises a universal spiritual quest

What part does God play in that spiritual
journey?
4. How would you sum up his approach in one
word?
Confrontational, conciliatory, challenging,
compromising, constructive, contradictory,
confessional?
5. In what ways could you link up with other
faith communities for the betterment of the
wider community?

Church, State and God

Read Romans 12:18—13:6:

Do all you can to live at peace with
everyone. Never try to get revenge; leave
that, my friends, to God's anger. As scripture
says: *vengeance is mine – I will pay them
back*, the Lord promises. But there is more:
*If your enemy is hungry, you should give
him food, and if he is thirsty, let him drink.
Thus you heap red-hot coals on his head*.
Resist evil and conquer it with good.

You must all obey the governing
authorities. Since all government comes
from God, the civil authorities were
appointed by God, and so anyone who
resists authority is rebelling against God's
decision, and such an act is bound to be
punished. Good behaviour is not afraid of
magistrates; only criminals have anything
to fear. If you want to live without being
afraid of authority, you must live honestly
and authority may even honour you. The
state is there to serve God for your benefit.
If you break the law, however, you may well

have fear: the bearing of the sword has its significance. The authorities are there to serve God: they carry out God's revenge by punishing wrongdoers. You must obey, therefore, not only because you are afraid of being punished, but also for conscience' sake. This is also the reason why you must pay taxes, since all government officials are God's officers. They serve God by collecting taxes.

Bearing in mind that Paul was writing about the Roman Empire under the infamous Nero it is remarkable that he calls the government officials 'God's officers' (literally, servants/deacons of God).

1. What does this reveal about Paul's attitude to the State?
2. How does this compare to the attitude of Jesus? Look up John 19:8–11.
3. To what extent do these two views inform our understanding of how God is at work in the community?
4. How far does the establishment of the Church of England hinder or enable the prophetic witness of the gospel?

A Hymn to the Kingdom

Come to the Lord
All those of the earth
Blind to your colour, seeing Christ;
In whom there is
No black no white,
Only the wounded and the weak;
Who at His cross in peace unite.

And there Christ tore all barriers down,
Curtains of iron and walls of hate
To make one race to grace His world.

You are the Lord
Of all the earth,
Eyes full of tears, our weeping God.
You gave your house
A place for prayer
For every race to worship You.
Make us your Church an open door
For strangers here and from afar;
Then let Your light shine through your tears
To dance new colours on one race.

(James Jones)

To be read by one person, after which a time of
silence can be kept. (These words can also be sung
to the tune 'Jerusalem'.)

Session 6

God in the World

with Myra Blyth

The Revd Myra Blyth is a Baptist minister from Scotland who holds a senior position in the World Council of Churches. She is based in Geneva and travels the world. As this Lent Course was planned it was felt that hers would be a distinctive contribution. Her world perspective gives to this brief course a dimension that takes us beyond the parochial. The neighbourhood of the local church has rightly been the focus of our reflection so far and the local Christian community has been the setting for this course for unless the Church lives locally it cannot grow internationally. But we need to lift our eyes beyond the boundaries of the parish and see what God is doing in other parts of his world.

I put it to Myra Blyth that, in spite of mass communication turning the world into a global village, many people are not interested in what is going on in the rest of the world. I asked her how we should respond to such parochialism.

I think it is about how we enable people to be interested and in what way we nurture that interest. For example, mass communication – it's clearly a tremendous blessing. We can enter into any part of the world so quickly, so instantly and see what is happening to people's lives. But unfortunately equally we exit that with the same speed and the same haste. So it gives us a rather warped view of what the world is really like. In the work I am involved in we are particularly trying to see ways in which to help people respond to human catastrophes around the world. For example, there was this traumatic earthquake in India. And in cool, or cold even, media terms this was almost a gift story because the media had been so preoccupied for months with this devastating situation in Bosnia that they had no other story to cover that was of equal drama. So, they rushed to India to cover the earthquake. However, three days after the earthquake took place, there was the siege of the Moscow parliament so the same media rushed to Moscow giving us the perspective on human catastrophe in India that it had come and it had gone. India was therefore the recipient of three days global solidarity. Now the question I think we as churches and as Christians have to ask is how can we responsibly respond to, and perceive, human need; not to become simply the victims of what we see on our celluloid screens.

The power of the media is phenomenal. Bob Geldof in his autobiography *Is That It?* recalls how during the famous Live Aid concert the phone-in system registering credit card donations broke down under the surge of calls that followed the screening of a video-clip of a single malnourished child trying and trying again to stand up on his little matchstick legs. But constant exposure to these powerful images can induce a compassion fatigue and a retreat from engaging with the suffering of the rest of the world.

I asked Myra whether being part of the worldwide Church enabled us to resist the temptation of cutting and running away from the problems others endured.

One obvious way that we can try to deal with our temptation to run is to think about the people rather than the problem itself, and to think about those people who are our partners on the other side of the world. The Church has a real chance where the secular world only has nameless faces. We have people that we know, whose names are known to us who belong to the Christian family and are our entry point into societies who are living with, rather than running away from, the problems. So it is the quality of our partnership that really gives us a possibility to stay with problems.

Myra's hope is that the unique relationship of partnership within the world-wide Church provides a different context for Christians to engage with the rest of the world. But I challenged her about the emphasis on partnership. Historically Christians in the West have seen themselves as the lady bountiful dispensing largesse. Such an image, however flawed, has been effective in channelling resources to churches in other countries. Does turning the tables and saying that churches in the West have as much to learn and to receive from Christians in other parts of the world not undermine and pull the rug from beneath the feet of those encouraging Christians to give more of themselves to world mission? In other words, why give if they've got as much to give?

I don't think it pulls the rug. It actually helps us to redefine and to learn the lessons of where mission work needed to move on from where it was. Mission work now is quite clearly not described as only one-way traffic, which it clearly was in its origins. It is a two-way traffic. It is, quite this – partnership. Partnership is both a receiving as well as a giving, and perhaps we need to continually emphasise this question of what does it mean to receive as well as to give. I am very taken by the challenge that came from the aboriginal woman Leila Watson, who said to a global gathering in the early 80s, 'If you, the rich world, have come to help us you are wasting your time but if you have come because your liberation is bound up with ours, then let's work together.' And it's a very strong challenge of 'mind your own business', if you think you have got the answers for us. I think the other end of that challenge is not only to recognise that our liberation is bound up with our partner, but that our liberation is something which is so urgent right now.

I met recently along with two or three other people from Europe. We met with a group of people from Latin America and we were each to present to the other group what the world looks like from where we live. And the Latin Americans were first. And they were so full of passion, of energy, of enthusiasm. From a continent that knows extensive poverty, they were vibrant with enthusiasm and with hope. You could feel amongst the Europeans a tremendous anxiety rising: 'It's going to be our turn very soon.' And there we were sitting in a row each with our prepared speeches. And we were so boring. And we were so lacking in energy and we were with this group for a week, and as the week went on, more and more the question emerged from us to them, 'Where do you get your hope from? Where do you get your energy from?' We were almost insulted. How could these people who have so little materially have the one thing we need – hope? And their answer was, 'We dream. We dream of Utopia.' This was not an answer that made any sense to us at the time because we have been educated not only not to express needs but dreams are things of children. Well, I think as time has gone on I have had a chance to reflect on what they were saying. But they had what we didn't have.

Myra is the director of the World Council of Churches' programme for sharing and service. She has been deeply affected in the course of her work by experiences of what God is doing in and through Christians in other parts of his world. When we met in London she was en route back to Geneva and full of stories of people who were shaping her life, like Pastor Nico.

Pastor Nico grew up in the Dutch Reformed Church in South Africa and was very much educated in that theology which affirmed a system whereby black and white are not ordained by God to sit together, to talk together, to live together. And Pastor Nico described how that was for him an unquestioning theology. A very, very nice man; a very, very committed pastor. And then one day he went and met Karl Barth in Germany. And Karl Barth said to him, 'Are you at peace in your country?' And he thought he meant in the environment. He said, 'Of course, we are quite free to move, to walk, to talk. There's no problem.' And Karl Barth said, 'No, but are you at peace in yourself?' And he said this was the end of the discussion – 'But I went home and that question has haunted me for the rest of my life.' And slowly over the years Pastor Nico, from being a top theologian in a very comfortable professorial chair, in a very good university, suddenly found himself having to

111

renounce everything and go and be the pastor in a township. And what moved me about his story was that he was not some radical from his early days. He was a basic, honest, middle of the road, good theologian; did what his dad said; lived in a very normal way. But then he said, 'Suddenly I had no option. I just had to renounce what I was doing.' But the naming of that was a very slow process. His story helped me because I think for many people the power of living with what you have received rather than moving to what you learn is extremely difficult.

The extraordinary events of South Africa's history have always brought to the fore the relationship of the Church to the State. In the past it has raised issues as to what extent Christians should be prepared to resist or disobey the dictates of the government. Some have seen the Church and the State as two independent spheres; others have argued that it is impossible to separate them out. At the root of the argument is a theological question about the nature of the Kingdom of God. Is the Kingdom the Church because, as Jesus said to Nicodemus, 'Unless a person is born from above he cannot see or enter the Kingdom of God' (John 3)? Or, is the Kingdom the world because as the Psalms proclaim, 'The earth is the Lord's and all that therein is.'

So often the answer to a theological question is 'yes' and 'yes'. The Kingdom of God is both the world and the Church. God rules over the whole earth therefore there is no territory nor human activity beyond his sovereignty; he is King over all the world which is therefore his Kingdom. The Kingdom of God is also the Church for this is the gathering of people from all corners of the earth who acknowledge personally the reign of God in Jesus Christ; they have entered into a personal relationship with the King and so make themselves the answer to their own prayer 'Your Kingdom come.'

Myra had her own insight into the nature of the Kingdom of God.

> The Kingdom of God is where we see God being broken, shared, received, celebrated. Now, that is too mystically put, but let me give you a story that for me explains it. I think it was Archbishop Oscar Romero in El Salvador who during his life was very much given to make pastoral visits to local churches. And on one occasion he visited a small town who had been greatly anticipating his presence. But when he arrived he found the villagers outside of the town – outside of the church, weeping. And he said, 'What is the problem?' And they pointed to the ground and they said, 'Look. Last night thieves entered the church, stole the reserved sacrament and look, they even threw the wafers on the ground.' And his reply to them was, 'Why are you surprised? Do you not know that the Body of Christ is trampled in the mud every day?' He brought the Kingdom of God right to them by helping them to see that those symbols that they were preserving were about something real that was happening outside, and that by seeing it and by feeling it, they were in touch with God and with the Kingdom.

Myra went on to illustrate further how she saw God's Kingdom being built.

I was visiting in India recently a group of women, nearly 500 women in a whole selection of villages in India – many of them are dahlit, i.e. untouchables. And these women have become the recipients of very, very small-scale loans – 50 dollars would be big-time; 10 dollars is more like it. And these women are being encouraged to set up small businesses. Now many of these women are single mothers; they have many children to look after; they have housing if they are lucky and they have no means, no access to any kind of resources except the money-lender. The money-lenders want them to stay in their pocket. These women are being trained to run a business. They are not regarded by the real world, as credit-worthy but in the name of Christ they are truly credit-worthy. They have dignity and they have the possibility with very, very small loans to run their own businesses and so I watched them. One woman was running a project of making packed lunches for the local factory. So she made whatever it was in her bowl; put it into leaves; folded up the leaves and tied them up; put them into a bucket and took them to the local factory. But she walked with her head high because she was now some-body who was self-sufficient. The Kingdom of God had arrived.

I pressed her about this understanding of the Kingdom. Nobody could deny the immense value of bringing dignity to these oppressed women. Furthermore, the righting of wrongs and the estab-lishment of a more just and merciful society are clearly in tune with the heart of God revealed in the history of salvation recorded in the Bible. But,

I asked, if we say that God is at work in any process where wrongs are being righted why should we then worry about actually bringing people to a personal faith in Jesus Christ and gathering them into the Church?

Christianity is clearly more than doing good. It is more than what is humanly possible, which is essentially why it is so important to name the name of Christ both in our actions and in our words. I believe that the Christian action is expressing to people who are in that kind of abject poverty that there is hope even where it appears to be hopeless, and that hope is based on exactly what Christ was trying to demonstrate in the way that he lived and died. Christ was demonstrating that we can live as if something more is possible than appears to be humanly the case. To live in the shadow of death, which is the normal human experience, is to submit to ever-decreasing possibilities. To dance to the song of the Resurrection is to admit to a world of ever-increasing possibilities. And that is not a trick of the mind. It is a simple step of faith which says – I know, or at least, I will live as if I know, that something more is possible. And so the woman that has no possibilities is encouraged by whatever means to live as if more is possible.

In conclusion, I brought Myra Blyth back to the local church and to the situation in which we find ourselves following this course in the local church. What practical advice could she suggest to enable us to realise the stories and ideals in our own situations?

I would rather say, what we need to do right

now is not to panic. I think that there is a tremendous feeling, when we look at the world, of compassion fatigue and panic. We think we don't know where it's going and we need to find a quick solution. But that's like the story of the mass media rushing in and rushing out. We don't need quick solutions. What we need is the spiritual maturity simply to allow God to do God's work. Christ was a very active leader for most of his life. But from the time at which Judas handed him over he was, and you can read it in Scripture, totally and utterly passive. He didn't do anything, according to John's Gospel he didn't even think any more. Everything was done to him. But that is actually saying to us that God is both an active and a passive God and that it is not any more wrong to be passive than to be active. We have to have at least a sense of waiting – allow the story, allow the gospel to move us rather than for us to feel the need always to make a plan – allow the gospel to take its own power and in the waiting discover how to listen, to listen to the partner on the other side of the world for whom we have the answer; to listen to the partner on the other side of the world who actually has the ability to address our need and to listen to what it is that we might be able to do that is beyond what we believe at this moment is possible.

The Global Village

1. What TV pictures have made you aware of the suffering of others?
2. What did you feel and how did you deal with these feelings?

3. Take the week's newspapers and cut out stories and pictures that contrast most with your own situation.

   Place these in the centre of the group on the floor and let each person speak about the contrast between the picture/story chosen and their own situation.

4. Bearing in mind Myra Blyth's comments, to what extent does belonging to the world-wide Church give you an opportunity of entering further into the situations of those you talked about in questions 1 and 3?

Partnership

Read 2 Corinthians 8:1–15:

> Now here, brothers, is the news of the grace of God which was given in the churches in Macedonia; and of how, throughout great trials by suffering, their constant cheerfulness and their intense poverty have overflowed in a wealth of generosity. I can swear that they gave not only as much as they could afford, but far more, and quite spontaneously, begging and begging us for the favour of sharing in this service to the saints and, what was quite unexpected, they offered their own selves first to God and, under God, to us.
>
> Because of this, we have asked Titus, since he has already made a beginning, to bring this work of mercy to the same point of success among you. You always have the most of everything – of faith, of eloquence, of understanding, of keenness for any cause, and the biggest share of our affection

– so we expect you to put the most into this work of mercy too. It is not an order that I am giving you; I am just testing the genuineness of your love against the keenness of others. Remember how generous the Lord Jesus was; he was rich, but he became poor for your sake, to make you rich out of his poverty. As I say, I am only making a suggestion; it is only fair to you, since you were the first, a year ago, not only in taking action but even in deciding to. So now finish the work and let the results be worthy, as far as you can afford it, of the decision you made so promptly. As long as the readiness is there, a man is acceptable with whatever he can afford; never mind what is beyond his means. This does not mean that to give relief to others you ought to make things difficult for yourselves; it is a question of balancing what happens to be your surplus now against their present need, and one day they may have something to spare that will supply your own need. That is how we strike a balance: as scripture says: *The man who gathered much had none too much, the man who gathered little did no go short.*

1. What examples can you think of from your own experience when an individual or a group have behaved like the churches in Macedonia?
2. What effect did this have on the recipient and on the giver?
3. St Paul cites Jesus as the example of how we should give. What incidents from the Gospels can you think of where Jesus gives us an example of how to receive from others?

118

4. What words in this passage most stress the concept of partnership?
5. What churches in other parts of the world are you, your church, your deanery etc. in partnership with?
6. What have you received from that partnership?

Peace and Shalom

1. To what extent does a society being at ease and at peace with itself depend on its people being at peace within themselves?
2. In Ephesians 2:11–18 Paul describes the social divisions between the Jews and the Pagans (the Gentiles).
   How does Christ make a difference to their relationship?
3. If the Kingdom of God is both the world and the Church how should this affect the way Christians relate to issues of justice and mercy?
4. In what way does your own personal relationship with Jesus Christ affect your attitude to global issues?

Resurrection

1. Myra Blyth sees the Resurrection of Jesus Christ as vitally important because it shows that there is hope beyond what is humanly possible.
   What experience do you have of seeing something happen that previously seemed impossible?
2. What small action could you and your group

take to live out the truth that 'God so loved the *world* . . .'?

Meditation

1. Place one of the newspaper pictures in an old tin in the centre of the room.
2. Let the group keep silence while they focus on the picture.
3. Place some bread in the tin with the picture.
4. Then read,

Then the King will say to those on his right hand, 'Come, you whom my Father has blessed, take for your heritage the kingdom prepared for you since the foundation of the world. For I was hungry and you gave me food; I was thirsty and you gave me drink; I was a stranger and you made me welcome; naked and you clothed me, sick and you visited me, in prison and you came to see me.' Then the virtuous will say to him in reply, 'Lord, when did we see you hungry and feed you; or thirsty and give you drink? When did we see you a stranger and make you welcome; naked and clothe you; sick or in prison and go to see you?' And the King will answer, 'I tell you solemnly, in so far as you did this to one of the least of these brothers of mine, you did it to me'. (Matthew 25:34–40)

5. The leader then takes the bread and shares it completely with the group so it is all eaten in silence.
6. The leader then lights the newspaper picture while the group watches in silence.
7. Then read,

120

Then it will be their turn to ask, 'Lord, when did we see you hungry or thirsty, a stranger or naked, sick or in prison, and did not come to your help?' Then he will answer, 'I tell you solemnly, in so far as you neglected to do this to one of the least of these, you neglected to do it to me'. (Matthew 25:44–5)

8. Say together the prayer on page 7.